Your New Restaurant

Praise For Vincent Mischitelli And *Your New Restaurant*:

"A great book! Restaurant management is a complex business, but Vincent Mischitelli has 'uncomplicated' the many nuances that make for success in the field."

> — *Robert F. Wickstrom*, Manager of Field Training and Development, Friendly Restaurants

"With Vincent Mischitelli's help, I was able to turn a $50,000 investment in a restaurant into a $200,000 sale—in less than one year!"

> —*James Taverno*, Former Owner, Marcelo's Restaurant, Worcester, Massachusetts

"Being in the business of having to review restaurants and hotels across the country, I found Mr. Mischitelli's book right on the money. He hits upon many of the qualities we look for in judging a restaurant."

> —*Fred Anderson*, KABC-TV News, Los Angeles, California

"Must reading for potential restaurateurs; reveals the hard facts that must be recognized before embarking on a business venture such as this. Your New Restaurant can help prevent costly mistakes. I highly recommend it."

> — *Donald Markey*, Assistant Vice President, Bank of New England

"Mr. Mischitelli's analytical systems work. He can show you the light at the end of the tunnel, whether you are dealing with product, payroll, administration, or personnel."

> — *Sharon Lallanzio*, Owner's Representative, Sheraton Leominster Hotel and Conference Center

Your New Restaurant

*All the necessary
ingredients for success*

Vincent Mischitelli

Adams Publishing
Holbrook, Massachusetts

Published by Adams Media Corporation
260 Center Street, Holbrook, MA 02343

ISBN: 1-55850-857-0

Printed in the United States of America

C   D   E   F   G   H   I   J

This publication is designed to provide accurate and authoritative information with regard to the subject matter covered. It is sold with the understanding that the publisher is not engaged in rendering legal, accounting, or other professional advice. If legal advice or other expert assistance is required, the services of a qualified professional person should be sought.
— From a *Declaration of Principles* jointly adopted by a Committee of the American Bar Association and a Committee of Publishers and Associations.

This book is available at quantity discounts for bulk purchases.
For information, call 1-800-872-5627.

Visit our home page at http://www.adamsonline.com

TABLE OF
CONTENTS

Chapter 9

INTRODUCTION

RECENT ESTIMATES ARE THAT EATING AND DRINKING ESTABLISH-
ments do over $150 billion worth of business in this country every year. Full-ser-
vice restaurants make up one of the largest segments of the overall food
business. Is there room for you in this exciting field? If you are willing to work
hard, work smart, and avoid the common mistakes made by others in the field,
the answer is yes.

Most banks consider restaurants high risk investments; lending institutions
often simply refuse to give loans to restaurants, and it's easy to understand why.
Over 80% of new restaurants are insolvent within five years (at least that's the
estimate a banker friend of mine made).

There is a paradox at work here, however. The restaurant industry has experienced a fantastic growth rate over the last few years. How then do we explain the poor survival rate of new establishments? I have a theory: bad
management. I believe that the people walking around new restaurants with the
word manager pinned to their lapels often lack the ability or willingness to follow a sound set of management principles, such as those outlined in this book. If
you want your restaurant to survive (and prosper) over those first crucial years,
the best thing you can do to put the odds in your favor is to learn the common
pitfalls, learn how to avoid them, and then put your knowledge into practice.
That's where this book comes in.

●　■　●

My father, who was in the retail business all of his adult life, opened a restaurant at age 58 and was quite successful. He faced many hurdles: he was an Italian immigrant, he had a tough time with the English language, and it was hard for him to explain things to other people who spoke only English. Nevertheless, he did well, and I learned a great deal from him (mostly by following his example).

Both he and my mother learned the restaurant business from the ground up. Sometimes there were conflicts between them about the business; I always tried to learn whatever I could from these episodes. For instance, my father could never convince my mother that portioning had to be uniform, no matter who was ordering the meal. When my mother worked in the kitchen and was given an order, she would always check to see who ordered the item. If two men, one large and one small, ordered the same entree, she would send out more food for the larger man than for his companion. She was only trying to be fair, but she probably wouldn't last long in a modern restaurant setting!

I worked for my parents while I was in high school and college; I worked hard and learned more and more every day. What they taught me formed the basis for my later career. Now, as a result of twenty years on my own as a professional in the industry, I can break down all the key factors that influence a restaurant's success into nine basic categories. They are:

- Location.
- Menu.
- Understanding and facilitating internal good will.
- Managing personnel.
- Fostering good public relations and knowing suitable advertising techniques.
- Systematizing inventory.
- Implementing a good purchasing system.
- Managing money.
- Maintaining the facility.

Let's move beyond failure and success rates for a moment. As a consultant, I can tell you with confidence that no matter what the bank's statistics have to say about you, if the factors I have mentioned are attended to, your restaurant will succeed. If they aren't, it won't.

Each chapter of this book is keyed to one of these topics. If you follow the advice in each chapter, and make sure to implement the ideas into your business's everyday operations, you will be successful.

Proceed through the book, chapter by chapter, and refer back to sections you feel merit further review. You will see results. (A brief side note is in order here on categorization: some might question why dining room furnishings are discussed in the chapter on menu planning. I believe that the customer's identification with the surroundings and his identification with the menu are so intimately related that they must be discussed together.)

A restaurant is a dynamic enterprise. If principles are adhered to, an organized, profitable establishment should be the result. If there is not a defined set of fundamental principles, chaos will rule and the establishment will fail. It is up to you to make sure your enterprise falls into the first category, and not the second. I hope and believe this book will help you in your efforts.

1

LOCATION

1

LOCATION

Worth

THE VALUE OF ANY REAL ESTATE DEPENDS TO A GREAT EXTENT ON location. Statistics comparing medium-sized houses in San Francisco (selling for $200,000) with similar houses in the Tennessee lowlands (selling for $110,000) are periodically published. The reason for the differences in value is location. Even within a city or a county, there can be a disparity in the value of similar houses. Socio-economic conditions, teaching institutions, proximity to amusement centers, availability of utilities, and closeness to the ocean, lakes, and mountains are all factors that contribute to the worth of a property.

There are some misconceptions about the cost of location. People do not always realize that the cost of land does not affect the cost of construction. As an example, let's assume that someone has architectural plans for a house and is trying to decide on a site. He has two lots in mind: one expensive, the other lower in price. Both plots are the same size, have the same kind of topography, and have the same geological make-up. One is in an area where lots sell for $10,000, the other in a location where lots sell for $40,000. It is important to remember that the house in the better locale is not going to cost 400 percent more to construct; the structural costs will be the same. Labor and material costs don't escalate because a house is in a better location. On the other hand, a house in the higher-priced area could be worth 50 percent more than if it were built on the cheaper-priced lot. Location is directly related to equity. The more a site is worth, the more the building on it will be worth.

Improvement costs will be the same, but their value is influenced by location. If someone buys a gallon of paint for $10, where he uses the paint will determine the net worth of his efforts.

When someone pays more for location, it is like buying a good racehorse. You pay for quality, but the cost of boarding and feeding are the same for any horse. It doesn't cost any more to feed Secretariat than it costs to feed a one-time winner. They both eat the same oats.

Location

Kitchen equipment, furnishings, and cosmetics cost the same for a restaurant regardless of location. Utilities, maintenance, labor, and products also cost the same when comparing different sites in the same general area. It costs just as much to repair a sink in a lousy location as it does in a good location.

Location is a major component of good will. A restaurant that is doing poorly (due to bad business practices), but is in a great location, can be sold very easily. A restaurant that is doing poorly in a bad location is seldom sold.

Let's look at elements that affect a location's value.

1. *Place.* Where it is. Is it the center of a large community or on the periphery of a populated area or on a heavily traveled road near a densely populated area? A restaurant has to have a population base from which to draw its customers.

2. *Parking.* It can be part of the property or a public parking lot in the vicinity of the restaurant.

3. *Accessibility.* If an establishment is located on land abutting a major highway, all of the traffic will drive right by, unless there is an exit off the highway and a convenient access road to the restaurant. Accessibility is crucial when evaluating location.

4. *Visibility.* People are greatly influenced by what they see. If a restaurant is not easily visible by passing motorists, the value of its location is greatly diminished even if it has other characteristics of good location.

5. *Infrastructure.* This relates to all of the connectors between buildings and the rest of the community. They include all of the utilities, roads, sewers, and transportation facilities. The infrastructure ties the community together by providing for common needs.

Value

Whether a property is purchased or leased, its cost should be determined by a real estate appraiser. This work is usually done by professionals who work for lending institutions or corporations involved in various kinds of leasing arrangements. A prospective restauranteur can find out what the rent for a facility should be by canvassing neighboring businesses. Even a professional appraiser compares to make his analysis.

Location influences the kind of menu that should be offered. Demographics (population studies) can tell a potential restaurant owner whether the type of menu he or she has in mind is suitable for a particular area. The site, the menu, and the type of customer must all be compatible. It might not be a good idea, for instance, to have a classic, expensive, suit-and-tie restaurant in a low-income community.

If all aspects of location have been properly researched, the entrepreneur can begin the planning stage in earnest.

2

MENU

2

MENU

Menu Planning

I BELIEVE THAT MENU PLANNING IS SO IMPORTANT THAT IT SHOULD be considered the core of restaurant development. It is difficult to order furnishings unless one knows the type of customer the menu is designed to attract.

Perhaps you are familiar with the expression, "Putting the cart before the horse." This is what many failed restaurateurs do with their menus. They generally form their menus around foods *they* enjoy. A novice coming into the business will often be heard saying, "I can't miss; I've got a hell of a menu." This proprietor has visions of overflow crowds: the menu will draw them in and he will be rich. This is like saying that it's easy to hit the lottery, all you have to do is pick the right numbers. However, the odds of doing so are a million to one. A restaurateur who does not organize and prioritize his restaurant planning with a system that includes all of the elements directly associated with the menu is bucking similar odds.

Your menu is very important and is one of the identifying traits of a restaurant. To plan a menu properly, one must consider the principles that give it a real consistency with all aspects of the establishment.

Suppose one walks into a beautifully decorated dining room with a very strict dress code; it is unlikely that the menu would be limited to fifteen varieties of hot dogs and draft beer. There are principles that should be followed to blend the menu harmoniously with the rest of the establishment.

The basic steps of menu planning are as follows:

1. Premenu Concerns

a. Identifying the customer and appropriate foods

b. Checking product availability and storage capacity

c. Learning profitability

d. Pricing and portioning

2. Menu Layout
   a. Color

   b. Logo

   c. Style of print

   d. Food descriptions

   e. Placement of food categories

3. Postmenu Concerns
   a. Hiring the right personnel

   b. Laying out service and cooking areas

   c. Writing clear food specifications

Premenu Concerns

The first item the menu planner must deal with is identifying the target audience. Who is going to be the average customer? Is she or he a member of the white tablecloth and silverware crowd? The up-and-coming professional? The average blue-collar worker? The upscale working couple, who eat out four to five times a week? Or the customer who enjoys a particular ethnic food? The answers to these questions determine the quality and type of food, the menu pricing, the number of entrees and the method of marketing.

The planner must consider, too, whether the customer will drive or walk to the restaurant. Menu planning for the customers who walk to restaurants usually occurs in large cities, amusement centers such as Disney World, large shopping plazas, or at large hotel resort areas such as Atlantic City. Generally the menus in these locations are limited and geared for quick turnover with luncheons served for four hours, and an average customer stay of half an hour. Seven to eight turns daily (in other words, seven or eight hours worth of capacity) is not unusual in these establishments. These customers almost always have a captive audience; that is, customers in the area for reasons other than eating.

For the drive-to facility, the menu planner must determine if the target audience is large enough to support the restaurant.

I did a consulting job for a man who wanted to open a restaurant with a fifties dine-and-dance theme. I asked why he chose that particular theme, and he answered, "It's great music, and there is nothing around here like it!" Even though I disagreed with the premise that it was great music, I asked him to hold off on the concept until I looked at the area more closely.

I found out that the age group he was targeting was the smallest of the groups within driving distance of his restaurant. Most of those people were born during the depression, when there was a very low birthrate. I also found out that the surrounding area had three establishments with a fifties dance theme in the previous ten years, all of which failed within the first four months of operation. There was a good reason there was nothing around there like it—there were not enough customers to support it.

I have a friend who could light a cigarette, throw it up in a tumbling motion with his tongue to a height of about three feet, and catch it with his lips, always with the filter side in. Once I remarked, "John, that is just amazing. I'll bet there aren't too many people in the world who can do something like that!" He replied, "Yes, but there aren't enough people in the world who would pay to watch me do it, so that I could make a living at it! There is just no call for it!" No matter how amazing or how good *you* think an idea for a menu seems, investigate first, and make sure there are customers who would support it to a degree that is profitable.

All menu-planning concerns should flow from the identification of the potential customer. Let's use the example of the family-style restaurant, where the average customer is a middle-class working person with a working spouse. They have children. I'll call this person "Average Working Person", and identify him or her as AWP. Next, let's put all considerations about the menu to AWP in the form of a questionnaire. (See Fig. 1)

Customer AWP

Appetizer Types	Appropriate	Comments
fried chicken wings	yes	appropriate
escargot	no	too exotic
Sandwiches		
lobster croissant	no	too expensive
ham and cheese	yes	routine family fare
Soups		
lentil soup	no	not apt to be a big seller
chicken soup	yes	most appropriate
Entrees		
haddock and fries	yes	popular food
broiled mackerel	no	unpopular and not easily available
Food quality		standard to choice
á la carte	no	
entrees with side dishes included	yes	
style of print		easily legible
menu style (color, etc.)		consistent with decor
pricing		moderate to low and competitive with similar places in the area.

FIGURE 1

These responses suggest that the average family is attracted to conventional foods (i.e., hamburgers are more popular than quiche). And this family is also looking for a moderately priced menu. So, if this is your target customer, your menu must lean toward popular food items at moderate prices. I am not suggesting that the average person doesn't like lentil soup, but that he or she is more apt to *buy* chicken soup.

When doing any analysis for a menu, keep up with the public's changes in food preferences. Even the perfect menu for AWP might have to be moderated after a few years.

Availability and storage

Once one has determined the target audience and has a proposed menu, there are more considerations to be made before actually printing the menu.

A planner must concern himself with the availability of the food that must be purchased. Would the buyer spend more time looking for the product than actually purchasing it? How accessible are the menu items? For example, if mackerel is being considered as an entree, one would have to know whether it can be purchased close by, from whom, whether weekly or seasonally, and so on.

Another concern is whether the kitchen is suited to store the goods that the menu requires. Is there proper refrigeration? Is there enough room for the equipment essential in the preparation of particular foods?

Understanding profitability

The main reason for being in any kind of a business is to make a profit. However, analyzing the profitability of particular items can be complicated. One must understand profit before pricing a menu.

If the cost of an item is $1.00 and the selling price is $3.00, the mark-up is 200%. In this case one would be pricing from the cost point of view. If the same item sold for $3.00 and its cost is $1.00, the cost would be 33% and the profit would be 66%. In both cases, the gross profit is $2.00. But in the first case the analysis is from the cost point of view; in the second case from the selling price position. In most restaurants the analysis is from the menu-selling price. For example, the percentage of food cost to food sales. Here's an example. 12-ounce sirloin entrees: $2.50 meat, potato 10¢, plus vegetable 25¢, and wrap around (the items that accompany the entree, such as bread and butter) 15¢, total cost $3.00. Menu price: $12.00. Food cost for the sirloin entree would be analyzed at 25%. This is ideal, but in most restaurants food costs run high due to spoilage, mistakes in preparation, pilferage, or poor purchasing.

One can analyze percentages, and it is very important to do so. But the bottom line is always actual dollar profit.

Let me tell you a story. There was a retailer in a particular location who was by far the most successful businessman around. He was not highly educated. His profits were always high and someone once asked what he attributed his success to. He answered, "Look, you buy something for a dollar and you sell it for five dollars. If you don't make at least that four percent, man, you shouldn't be in business." Don't argue with success! There are situations when analyzing strictly by percentages gives a false impression of the actual profit. This fellow didn't know what percentages meant; he just made tons of money.

Let's try to get a little more insight into the relationship between percentage and profit.

Assume that two customers are standing in line, ready to check out at a candy store. Sally is buying a candy bar that sells for 20¢. Ann is buying a box of chocolates that sells for $8.00. The store owner turns to one of his friends, and says, "I wish I could sell more of those candy bars. I make a fortune on them. One costs me 2¢ and I sell it for 20¢. I make 900% on that item. But on the box of chocolates I make nothing. It costs me over $6.00 and I sell it for $8.00. I only make 33%."

Yes! At first glance, 900% profit looks much better than 33% profit. But actually he made only 18¢ on Sally and almost $2.00 on Ann. This point is important in understanding restaurant profitability. If Sally and Ann are sitting in a dining room, they are using part of the real estate for a particular length of time; that is, they are occupying a table and two chairs for the duration of their stay. While they are seated, no one except Sally and Ann can buy anything from that particular square footage. And if Sally is true to her form, as shown in the candy store, and orders a cup of coffee and a muffin—total profit 90¢—our only hope is that Ann orders a full-course meal with all the trimmings.

For another comparison, let's assume that eight people enter a restaurant at the same time and sit at two tables. At one table, four people order soup and sandwiches, with food cost at 25%, but a gross profit of $1.25 per customer. At the other table, four people order prime rib, which has a food cost of 43%, but a gross profit of $3.50 per customer. At the soup-and-sandwich table, the gross profit is $5.00, as compared to $14.00 at the prime rib table. There is a $9.00 difference between them, even though both tables take up the same amount of space. The astute owner would rather have a roomful of people eating prime rib, with a lesser markup, than a roomful of soup and sandwich eaters, with a greater markup. Remember, you don't take percentages to the bank. You take cash. That's the bottom line! The important thing is the amount of money you earn.

Pricing and Portioning

All of the analysis so far refers to gross profit. Net profit, on the other hand, is the bottom line after the total cost of sales and operating expenses has been deducted. In pricing the menu, there is an assumption that the restaurant has already projected an operating budget; that is, the cost of the mortgage or lease, labor, insurance, taxes, utilities, etc. Before actually pricing a menu, read this book all the way through, paying special attention to chapter 7, which covers operating budgets.

Many successful restaurants use a prime cost analysis when setting up their menu or evaluating costs. Prime cost is the combined expenditure for product and labor. A good prime cost percentage should be in the 60s. Thirty-two percent product costs and 31% total labor cost equal 63% prime cost.

In general, most restaurants must have food costs under 35% of menu price to be successful. In some locations, due to the high cost of real estate, food costs must be under 20% of food sales. Beverage costs are generally 14% to 18% of beverage sales in high-rent districts.

If a restaurant has an operating budget that can support a 30% food cost structure, it can be competitive and yet still have high gross sales.

The first step is defining the portion size of each item on the menu, and as accurately as possible predicting the portion costs. This can be done by asking for priced-out commodity sheets from the vendors in your area. If the average price of sirloins is $3.50 per pound after trimming, and the menu advertises 12-ounce broiled sirloin, the portion price is $3.50 divided by 16 ounces in a pound, which equals approximately 22¢ per ounce. Multiply by 12 (for a 12-ounce portion), and the cost is $2.63 per steak portion. This type of math should be done for every single item on the menu including packets of butter, sugar, etc.

Once fairly accurate portion costs have been estimated, one can commence with a formula that leads to the ideal 30% food cost. Cost of food and setting divided by 30% equals the optimal menu price although you can adjust the figure upward slightly to reach certain "price points" if you wish.

Let's use the example of the sirloin steak entree above, and assume that all of the pricing has been done for the wrap around. Sirloin steak (12 oz.) $2.63 + potato (4 oz.) 13¢ + vegetable (3 oz.) 15¢ + bread 15¢ + butter 15¢ + placemat and napkin 11¢ + steak sauce (1 oz.) 4¢ = $3.36. The cost of the entree ($3.36), divided by .30 = $11.20. One should always adjust the menu price upward after the ideal price has been computed. $11.20 can go up to $11.50, but not downward to $10.95.

If a chef, restaurant manager, or food-and-beverage manager feels hesitant about performing the mathematical formulas mentioned above, it would be wise to hire outside help, such as an accountant. Menu pricing is very important to the success of a restaurant.

MENU LAYOUT

Things to avoid

Once food items, portions, and menu pricing have been determined one can set up the actual menu layout. Clarity is the number one consideration in both the layout of the menu and the euphemisms that describe each item. Over the years, I've noticed the following results from menus that were either poorly laid out, or with unclear entree descriptions.

Bad Placement. This results in people taking a long time to order because the general categories are not well organized. *From the Fryer* or *From the Grill*, for instance, can lead to trouble. Such a menu typically mixes appetizers with entrees. If the item is an appetizer, list under APPETIZERS and then identify whether it is fried, broiled, baked, etc. Too often when the menu layout is wrong, you can hear customers at one table asking, "Where do you see that on the menu?" This kind of reaction will not help turn tables over to new, enthusiastic customers on the regular basis you'd like. Customers who are confused and lingering due to bad menu information are not happy people.

Unclear entree descriptions. Too often I've seen waitresses standing over tables giving monologues trying to describe entrees. It is good to have knowledgeable waitresses who can describe items, but in many cases the reason an explanation has to be given is that the menu description is unclear.

It's good to use euphemisms in selling your menu items but they have to be carefully written, so as not to obscure a clear, accurate understanding of what the food is.

> Customer: "What's that?"
>
> Waitress: "Lamb's Tongue!"
>
> Customer: "I didn't order *that*, did I?"

When the platters are returned to the kitchen it is an angry chef who will have to deal with them. There must be reference to the generic name of the food. If it is duck, call it duck.

Inefficient phrasing. Then there is the menu that has a complete paragraph following each food item. In this case, customers look like they are in a library, spending more time reading than dining. One must be as efficient and concise as possible when describing items on a menu.

Unclear, inaccurate, and inefficient menu writing will cost a restaurant traffic, waste, embarrassment, service, and ultimately, profit.

Things to include

A well-planned menu should have

1. Color and logo consistent with the restaurant decor.

2. Print that is legible and consistent with decor.

3. Food descriptions that are clear, concise, and efficient.

4. Reasonable layout with food grouped by category.

Appetizers	**Entree**
Chicken Fingers	Baked Haddock
Shrimp Cocktail	Stuffed Shrimp
Fried Mushrooms	Boneless Chicken
Fried Zuccini	Sirloin Steak
Salads	**Desserts**
Garden Salad	Chocolate Mousse
Antipasto	Cheesecake
Chef Salad	Carrot Cake Puddings
Soup	
Minestrone	
Chicken	
Seafood Chowder	

FIGURE 2

Once all of this is done, send it to a reliable printer who has had experience with menus.

Postmenu Considerations

Finalizing a menu brings us to other concerns.

1. Hiring the appropriate chef, prep cooks and line cooks.

2. Hiring the appropriate service people.

3. Proper layout of the service area.

4. Proper layout of the kitchen.

5. Writing a food specification manual for the buyer, kitchen staff, and receiver.

Hiring appropriate kitchen staff

Your chef should have familiarity and background with the particular foods on your menu. He or she should also have an enthusiasm for working with your restaurant's particular style of entrees. I have often walked into the kitchen of a restaurant that does high volume, quick turns only to find that the chef is unhappy and claims, "Man, I don't belong here. I'm a great gourmet chef. I belong in one of the fanciest restaurants in the Big Apple!!!" He *doesn't* belong there. His attitude will crush the morale of the other employees and may lead to the demise of the establishment. Prep cooks and line cooks should also be hired with regard for the menu. Some are great with high-priced menus that require fancy garnishes, time-consuming preparations, and precise food placements; others are better at dealing with a fast-paced kitchen where volume output is important.

Appropriate wait staff

For some waitresses and waiters the slow, deliberate diner is not someone they like to deal with. I've interviewed many waitresses who were working in high-priced establishments, but who quit to work in a fast-paced environment. These people say that they were making good money, were happy with the management, but that there just wasn't enough action to suit them. On the other hand some servers are great conversationalists, are meticulous, and very deliberate, and have a demeanor that is not at all appropriate for an action-packed dining room. During an interview, most applicants will tell you what their particular talents are, if you ask them.

Proper layout of service area

The type of menu will affect

1. the proper positioning of the host or hostess. There should be reasonable space for customers waiting to be seated.

2. the proximity of the prepared food once the waitress or waiter has entered the kitchen for a completed order.

3. the concern for wait staff whose sections are furthest from the kitchen.

4. proper table distribution.

The reservation desk should be situated so that it is accessible to both waiting customers and wait staff. Customers have walked out because the hostess did not properly inform a waitress about a table she had just seated. Generally, these customers never come back to the establishment again. Therefore, it is essential that a good deal of thought be given to the placement of the reservation desk. The hostess must be able to communicate with guests who are waiting to be seated.

A partition should be set up to divide the waiting guests from those who are already dining. In restaurants where no such partition exists, I find myself enjoying my food only to feel the glances of the waiting patrons. Then I feel guilty: here I am stuffing my face, while they are still near the door, famished. Every dining room is different so every manager has to be creative in assuring that host or hostess communication and customer comfort are achieved.

I always count steps in planning service areas. My concern is how far a waiter or waitress has to go once he or she enters the kitchen area. I believe that this is very important. If the waitress station in the kitchen is five feet farther from the main dining area than it should be, the result is slower service and a more tired and less exuberant service staff. A good planner allows enough room to avoid a crowded condition when the staffers are picking up their orders, yet still minimizes steps.

Carrying a large tray filled with food for a distance of fifty feet is not an easy chore. Wait staff who have sections farthest from the kitchen should be given extra consideration. One way to help them is by providing a straight path to their section by creative table planning. Thought should be given to strategically placing more tray stands in these areas. I have not taken a scientific poll, but it is my experience that more of the embarrassing accidents (such as dropping platters of food) occur in these areas.

If at all possible, an extra service person—such as a bus boy or food runner—should be stationed in these locations. It is often advantageous to place your most talented service people in these areas and give them pay commensurate with the added responsibility.

In addition, the styles of the tables and chairs, and the method of placement, are directly related to the type of menu and restaurant they are intended to service. Besides esthetic considerations, seating plans are affected by handicap barrier laws, fire exits, the number of covers that are expected in order to meet gross income projections and customer and staff mobility.

In a high-volume restaurant where the prices are low to moderate, there might be a need for tables to be set relatively close together in order to maximize the number of clients. In a more upscale silver-and-crystal establishment, more distance might be required so that the customers (who stay for relatively longer periods of time and whose checks can be quite substantial) can feel comfortable about their space.

The type of restaurant dictates the kind of spacing and the types of tables and chairs that will be needed. One must assess the kind of customer turnover required for profitability in order to buy appropriate furnishings. Booths, booth-and-chair combinations, round tables, square tables, and oblong tables are some of the settings that make up the floor plans of dining rooms. Some restaurants have varied seating with several of the table shapes listed above.

In terms of space, the oblong table is the most efficient if two settings are placed on each of the long sides of the table (when seating a table of four). On the smaller oblong tables for two, the settings should be opposite each other on the short sides of the table. Circular tables are usually more efficient than square tables if the seating distance between two settings on opposite sides are exactly the same.

Booths are very efficient when they are all filled up; however, they are stationary, cannot be adjusted for bigger groups and cannot be broken down for smaller groups. They do offer customers a great deal of privacy; there are those who will not go to a restaurant unless it has booths. Restaurants that cater to families and larger groups might have table plans that allow for table movements to adjust to any size group (even ten or more). The larger oblong table should be a common fixture in this type of dining area. Tables should always be set up with serviceability in mind, regardless of the style or type of potential customer. Measure the room and establish the style of menu and type of prospective customer. Then begin shopping for furniture and planning seating arrangements. (See Figs. 3 and 4.)

Proper layout of the kitchen

"There can be no angrier man upon the face of the earth than a tired line cook in a busy restaurant, on the night of the Sabbath, in a kitchen that was planned by an architectural idiot!"

In the more than thirty years that I've either been directly or indirectly involved with restaurant kitchens and kitchen employees, the well-planned facility has been the exception rather than the rule.

Most kitchens are divided into four basic areas: the prep area, the line cook section, the dishwashing area, and the salad prep room.

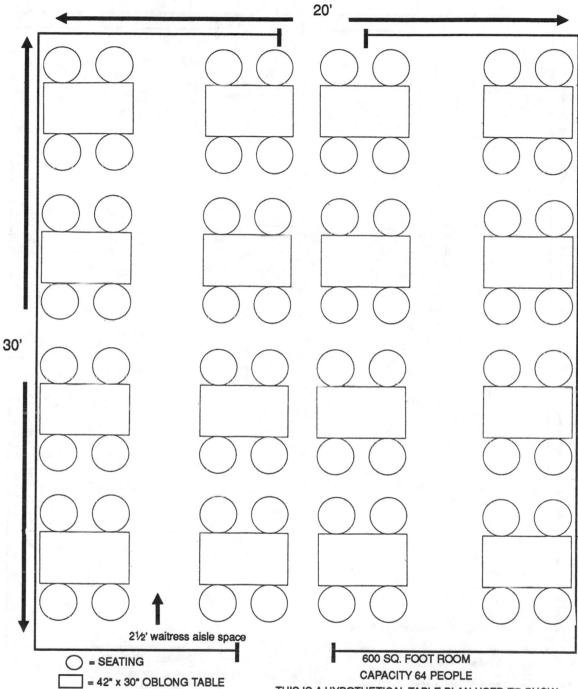

20'

30'

2½' waitress aisle space

◯ = SEATING

▭ = 42" x 30" OBLONG TABLE

600 SQ. FOOT ROOM
CAPACITY 64 PEOPLE
THIS IS A HYPOTHETICAL TABLE PLAN USED TO SHOW
SHAPCE EFFICIENCY OF THE OBLONG TABLE, WHEN TABLES
ARE PLACED IN CONFORMING ROWS. THIS IS NOT MEANT TO
BE USED AS A PLAN FOR ACTUAL TABLE ARRANGEMENTS.
FIGURE 3

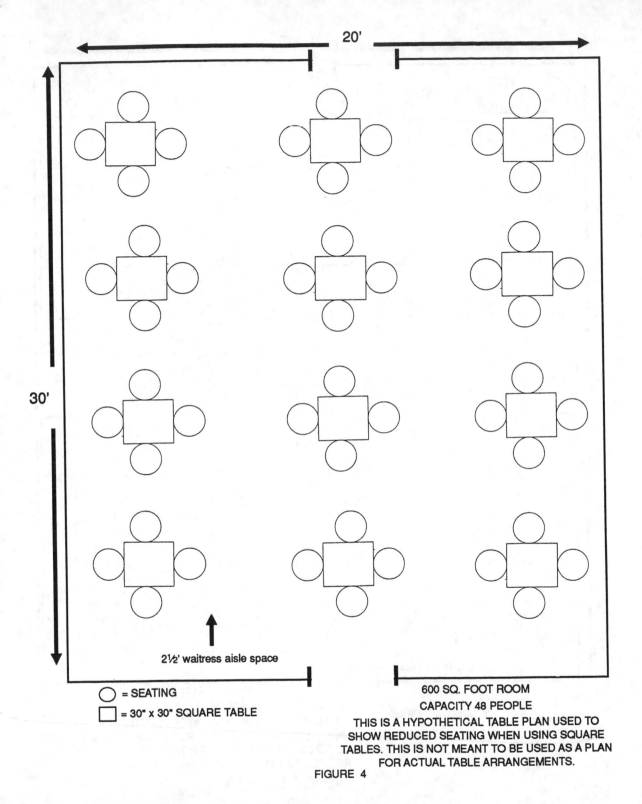

20'

30'

2½' waitress aisle space

○ = SEATING
☐ = 30" x 30" SQUARE TABLE

600 SQ. FOOT ROOM
CAPACITY 48 PEOPLE
THIS IS A HYPOTHETICAL TABLE PLAN USED TO
SHOW REDUCED SEATING WHEN USING SQUARE
TABLES. THIS IS NOT MEANT TO BE USED AS A PLAN
FOR ACTUAL TABLE ARRANGEMENTS.
FIGURE 4

Prep area

The preparation area is where vegetables are cut, meats are trimmed, sauces are made, baking and broiling of large cuts of meats (such as whole ribs or roasts) occurs, and homemade soups and desserts are prepared. If this area has enough room for the chores mentioned above, its location is not absolutely crucial in determining serviceability of the restaurant. However, efficiency considerations are essential when placing equipment in this area. Give your prep staff enough room for comfort, at the same time minimizing the number of steps they must take. There is a delicate balance here, but common sense should help you identify it. The most complex kitchen to set up is the multidirectional. This kitchen is set up to serve different rooms. It is generally located in the center of a facility, with the prep area central to the kitchen. In a restaurant with a single dining area the prep area is behind the line cook stations.

Some of the essential equipment for preparation include stainless steel prep tables (number and size will vary with restaurant type); cutting boards; a broiler; ovens big enough for twenty-pound cuts of meat; a sink deep enough to hold a sixty-quart pot; cutlery adequate for filleting and cutting fish, meat, and vegetables; ladles; spatulas; large commercial spoons and forks; an automatic slicer; a mixer; a food processor; a stove with large burners for oversize pots; and refrigeration for bulk foods (such as a walk-in refrigerator). If it is impossible to fit a walk-in in the prep area, it should not be very far away.

Ovens and stoves should be placed in one line and all the other major equipment in an opposite line, with a four-foot aisle between them. With this setup, a chef can prepare a roast on the prep table and put it in an oven with no difficulty. Pots can be hung overhead. A shelf or shelves can be installed above the prep table so that all spices are easily reached.

Line cook area

Here again the concern should be maneuverability. Line cooks don't like to work in cramped quarters, nor do they like to walk too far to assemble their orders. Remember, line cooks work under extreme pressure when the restaurant is busy. They come in contact with servers, who are in direct contact with customers. Good kitchen layout will minimize anxiety.

The menu will dictate the exact equipment used in this area. For example, a steak house may need an extensive broiler system. The equipment found in the line section should include a stove, an oven, a broiler, a fryolator, a microwave oven, a grill, a refrigerator, a freezer, a set-up table, a sandwich unit, and a waitress table with heating lights. The refrigerator and freezers should be set up next to or immediately across from the appropriate cooking unit. (The freezer containing frozen french fries, for example, should be near the fryolators, and the refrigerator containing meats should be close to the grill and broiler.)

Whenever equipment is being considered for any part of the kitchen, the first step is to measure the available space. If the equipment does not fit properly no amount of planning will do. When ordering equipment, consider height, width, and depth. Height is the distance from the floor to the top, including legs. Width is the distance from left to right, when one is facing the equipment. Depth is the distance from front to back. Many people confuse width and depth and end up buying equipment that will not fit their kitchen.

Dishwashing area

In today's kitchens, old-style manual dishwashing setups are virtually unheard of. Automatic dishwashers are essential in a high-volume establishment. It is necessary to buy a commercial washer built for heavy-duty use: the home variety will not do.

The wash area must be close to the exit with room for full bus carts. It must be close to a kitchen exit for garbage disposal and close to the line cooks so that clean dishes can be easily restocked. This all sounds difficult but is usually accomplished easily.

The dishwashing setup usually runs perpendicular to the line cook aisle. It doesn't have to be a large area but consideration should be given to the space required for bus carts, the dishwasher, and an area for stacking the clean dishes.

The salad area

Produce spoils easily, so the salad area should be close to the walk-in refrigeration unit. The proximity of refrigeration assures crisper, fresher salads, and protects against waste. Servers must have ready access to this area since salads are served more than any other food. The line cooks should be able to communicate easily with the salad preparer so that orders can be placed in the correct chronology. Proper placement of the salad area saves time and money—and keeps customers happy.

FOOD SPECIFICATIONS

Food specs, of course, are related to menu pricing and portioning, treated earlier in this chapter. They deal with the quality of the bulk food to be ordered (sometimes specific to brands and origin) and the method of preparation of each item.

The specifications relate to portioning, exact seasoning, cooking time, chronology of preparation, and the way each platter is set up. They are similar to recipes, except that they describe the preparation of single servings. Preparation of processed foods such as soups and sauces are also described in the food specifications.

Good food specs should

1. Be thorough, with every item mentioned.

2. Be clear and concise as to the methods of preparation.

3. Have exact ingredients with precise measurements and weights listed.

4. Be clearly legible.

5. Be organized in a booklet or binder with numbered pages covered with clear plastic to protect the pages from tearing or soiling.

6. Be reproduced in sufficient quantity for your staff.

A booklet of food specifications is useful to all employees of a restaurant with the exception of service staff. Chefs, prep cooks, line cooks, salad makers, buyers, inventory controllers, receivers, office personnel dealing with invoices, and management should have access to food specification information.

The specification booklet should deal with all bulk inventory products and describe food prep and portioning. Organize it clearly and logically into two main sections addressing those two issues.

Itemized products

The bulk section is generally used by the buyer, who buys foods of specific quality, and the receiver, who checks to ensure that that specific quality was sent by the vendor. The *USDA Meatbuyers Guide* is helpful in both writing the specs and in the buying and receiving process. The United States Department of Agriculture and most institutional food purveyors sell the Guide.

Leave a little room for deviation on the buyer's part. If there is too much specificity by name brand, the buyer will not be able to deal with salespeople effectively. If the specs call for X amount of choice sirloin and there is a company that has a tremendous deal on Y amount of choice, this change can be profitable. In this case, the buyer and the chef can get together to figure out a projected yield and do what is best for the restaurant. The quality of meat is not affected by this change. The customer will still be eating a delicious piece of steak.

Commodity pamphlets, which may be obtained from salespeople and distributors, can help in the writing of specifications for all canned goods, frozen items, boxed pastries, produce, dairy products, poultry, and bread. The specs should clearly specify acceptable brand names, packer codes, grades, yield codes, and sizes. For example, several brands of canned green beans might be acceptable. In other cases one might like the product labeled under the distribution name. In some cases, the distributor could be the packer.

Grading can be done by terms such as Grade A or fancy, which usually tell the restaurant that this is the best item packed under a particular brand label. Domestic might be used to show grade, but it is a term that can have many meanings. The writer of the specs should specify which grades are acceptable, and should work this out with the chef.

Packers might use differing terminologies when describing yield codes. Canned vegetables can be labeled by weight, water weight, or count of vegetables. For example, the yield could read net weight 5 lbs, 3 oz. or water weight 3 lbs., or 500/550 count. The preference for can size usually has to do with usage as prescribed by the menu. For the restaurant relying primarily on canned vegetables, the larger #10 cans should be used. For the restaurant that prides itself on freshly cooked vegetables, smaller #5 cans can be used to supplement soups or garnishes, or in fillers for foods such as stuffed tomatoes.

Here again, menu dictates all that will be in the specs for canned vegetables. The importance of a well-organized and thorough menu cannot be overemphasized.

Meat descriptions in the specs should be especially carefully written, because meats are among the costliest items purchased. Yield, grade, and size are all important considerations. The yield number refers to the amount of fat that surrounds the meat. The lower the number, the less fat. The generally accepted range is from Y-1 to Y-5. The grade refers to the federal stamp, which appears as a blue mark on the fat of the meat. These grades run from Prime (the best) to Standard. Most restaurants use USDA Choice. Some places use "no-rolls," which have no government inspection markings on the meat. In this case the meat has been inspected but the packer has chosen not to have it graded.

The *USDA Meat Buyer's Guide* can be of great help in both standardizing the meat to be procured and identifying items. This information should be part of the itemized descriptions written into the food specs.

Produce purchasing in some parts of the country (especially northern areas) can be expensive and difficult in the colder months. However, every effort must be made to write produce specifications that can be reasonably adhered to. Lettuce specifications should include the type (i.e., iceburg, romaine, Boston, etc.), count per case (12 or 24), trimmed or untrimmed style, and a minimum acceptable weight per case to insure consistency.

Potato specifications should include type, count per box (usually 90 or 100 count for baker's, and far less for chef's), and the area of origin, such as Idaho or Maine.

In the northeast, tomatoes are usually 6 x 6 size, with about 70 to 75 per 20-pound box. One should use natives and vine-ripened tomatoes when possible.

Specifications should be written for all food products used and made available to the chef, the buyer, the inventory controller, and the office staff.

Specifications for food preparation

The second part of the spec book deals with portions, recipes, and presentation, and should be written by the chef. Ingredients, portioning, preparation method, and presentation of every menu item should be completely described. This will assure both consistency and profitability. The kitchen staff should memorize the specs.

On the menu an item might read,

Chicken Teriyaki
Broiled boneless breast of chicken, marinated in our own teriyaki sauce, served with salad, choice of potatoes, and vegetable. $6.95

In the specification booklet Chicken Teriyaki should be listed in the same order as it appears in the menu, so that it can be found easily by the cooks.

The specs would list all of the ingredients and portions and then list the chronology of preparation and presentation.

> Boneless, skinless breast of chicken, 6 ounces, previously marinated for a minimum of 1½ hours; 5 ounces french fries or 100 count baked potato; 5-ounce tossed salad with 1 ounce dressing; two slices bread; ½ teaspoon sprinkled parsley; 4

ounces vegetable of the day; garnish with one slice tomato; lettuce underliner (2½" x 2½").

The preparation specs might read:

> Cook chicken on each side for about 4 minutes or until firm and cooked through. When chicken is placed on broiler be sure salad is being delivered to customer. Remove chicken when ready and place it on left side of 12-inch platter. Place potato to the right and vegetable to the lower middle. Garnish should be placed at the upper middle.

A good photo or drawing should be made. A completed plating should be on the spec sheet so that cooks and garnishing people know exactly what the product must look like when it is presented to the customer. (See Fig. 5)

There are various ways to describe the placement of food. For example, a chef might refer to the top of the platter as 12, just like the hours of a clock, thereby making the right side 3, the bottom 6, and the left side 9. In another establishment north, east, south, and west may be used. Whatever the method used, it is always from the point of view of the customer. Therefore, in the example used above, the main food item would be either bottom, south, or 6 o'clock with respect to the customer. The garnish would always be furthest away from him, or north, top, or 12 o'clock.

The recipe section of the specification booklet should contain a chapter on all in-house preparation and processing procedures. This includes all homemade items (such as salad dressings, sauces, and soups), and special entrees (such as meatloaf, lasagna, or large roast cooking and seasoning). Consistency is vital, and is a very important part of customer satisfaction. Haddock without seasoning will generally taste the same regardless of where it is purchased. What makes a piece of haddock taste great is the cheese sauce or the stuffing prepared by the staff. Therefore, it is crucial that specs ensure that the sauces and stuffing that accompany the entree are always top-notch. Care and consistency in preparation are important characteristics of a successful restaurant.

As this chapter has demonstrated, menu planning is not easy. The exact chronology will vary, depending on the size and type of the restaurant. For example, in a small restaurant the menu planner, chef, owner, manager, and

MENU ENTREE

BAKED HADDOCK

INGREDIENTS

(1)   8 oz. fresh haddock
1½ tbls. prepared crumb mix
1½ tbls. butter
ground parsley

(2)   baked potato 100 count
or
3 oz. french fries

(3)   3 oz. serving of vegetable of the day

(4)   fresh pasley—lemon wedge

PREPARATION

(1)   place haddock in #8 stain dish

(2)   sprinkle crumbs over the haddock

(3)   cover crumbs with butter, place in
baking oven 380˚, cook for
9 minutes

Place: stainless dish with
haddock at south on platter
oval dish
potato at west
vegetable at east
lemon and parsley
garnish north

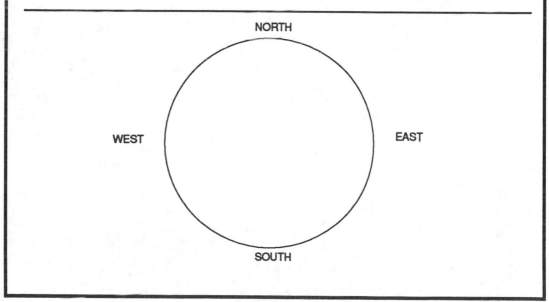

FIGURE 5

specifications writer might be the same person! There are three essential principles of menu planning.

1. Identifying the potential customer.

2. Writing a menu that will service the customer and will be profitable to the establishment.

3. Determining the best way to service the customer.

Sound simple? Try it!!

3

INTERNAL SYSTEMS THAT INFLUENCE GOOD WILL

3

INTERNAL SYSTEMS THAT INFLUENCE GOOD WILL

Word of mouth

THERE IS A COMMON PHRASE THAT IS HEARD IN AND OUT OF THE business community: "The best advertising is by word of mouth." How does a restaurant owner influence word-of-mouth advertising? He can't go around telling people to tell other people! The hope is that a favorable impression will somehow make its way through the desired audience once a restaurant has established a solid reputation and a certain amount of good will.

Good will can be evaluated from different points of view. A prospective buyer equates good will with location and gross amount of business, but good will can also mean favorable community relations.

Achieving popularity through a gradual process of people spreading the good word, is one of the most effective and tried-and-true forms of restaurant marketing. This kind of good will only takes place when the internal workings of the establishment encourage it.

What is the customer thinking? Before trying to understand the elements that foster good will, let's step back, try to be subjective and relate to the customer's psyche.

Have you ever been in a restaurant and asked yourself, "What on earth am I doing here? I could be home watching the game or a movie!" Certainly, eating in a restaurant is not a necessity. Most folks have food in their homes. With a microwave it's extremely easy to put a passable meal together. Just a little effort saves the hassle of getting into a car, driving five miles, parking the car, waiting to be seated, waiting for the check, and driving back home.

There must be something rewarding about dining out, however, because people are eating in restaurants more frequently. An astute entrepreneur would ask, "Why?"

Many attribute this phenomenon to the large numbers of families in which both husbands and wives are breadwinners. I believe that this is only part of the explanation. Much of the growth in the food service industry is the result of good competition and creative marketing. Just look at the expansion in the long-distance telephone industry since the breakup of Ma Bell. Competition has increased promotional efforts. Likewise, the restaurant industry is its own prime motivator. Good competition results in better restaurants and increased marketing. If there were just one restaurant in the world, it would be empty.

For a restaurant to establish good will it must give a certain satisfaction and joy to its customers. Once a customer walks through the door, the internal dynamics of the restaurant must be in place to please him or her.

A customer once asked me to sit down with him. He proceeded to tell me how to run the restaurant. I politely listened to what he was saying but inside my heart was telling me "What the hell does this guy know? Why is he bothering me?" And then it suddenly dawned on me: he knew everything, he was the customer. All too often managers ignore the opinions of the clientele. The opinions of customers (if they are properly sorted out and placed in the proper perspective) can be a valuable source of information for possible menu changes, seating rearrangements, or any other factors that could improve reputation.

Good will is generated by

1. good food

2. good service

3. good atmosphere

4. consistent scheduling, and

5. adequate sanitation practices.

GOOD FOOD

Today's restaurant patron has very sophisticated food preferences. This patron eats many meals away from home and has become critical in evaluating foods. One must insure that the food coming out of the kitchen is consistently of high quality to satisfy a tough critic such as this.

If a restaurant has a reputation for lousy food, it is going to go out of business. This is simply inevitable (unless, of course, the establishment is a front for something unsavory, like a bookie joint). Food taste, quality, and consistency are essential for a restaurant's success. Hiring a good chef is extremely important: the chef is directly responsible for the quality of the food and its acceptance by the clientele. What qualities should a manager look for when hiring a chef? He or she must have a good reputation as a cook, good qualities as a manager, and be an individual who has a consistent employment record.

Good cook

A chef who makes delicious foods and has a good method of presentation is usually well known throughout the restaurant community. One generally hears about a good chef or cook in much the same manner one hears about a good restaurant: through word of mouth. A manager should contact former employers before making a hiring decision. Hire a chef who is consistent with the menu and theme of the restaurant. A gourmet chef might not be suitable for an Italian kitchen.

Personally, I prefer to stay away from prima donas. These are the chefs who claim to have cooked at the White House or for famous celebrities. I have an irrational fear of temperamental egocentrics who walk around kitchens with sharp knives. I once hired one of those patronizing types who demanded big bucks because he was so artistic. He carved great-looking ice sculptures, but his food turned out to be terrible.

Culinary art schools can be a source for staffing a kitchen. Most of the graduates have acquired knowledge of good food preparation and presentation.

Managerial qualities

The chef must be able to get along with his staff and service people. The mechanics of an efficient kitchen require organization and cooperation. The chef should be a catalyst in this regard. He or she must have sufficient management skills to coordinate the kitchen efforts.

Too often, cooks and chefs take their frustrations out on service personnel. Waitresses must come out of the kitchen with smiles on their faces, not tears in their eyes.

Employment history

The third consideration in hiring a chef is his or her employment record. If someone has had four jobs in three years, beware! This type of employee will work for awhile and usually leave without notice. He or she will lend instability to the establishment.

A chef is vitally important to the restaurant, so hire the best you can get. If this means a few thousand dollars more per year, do it! A restaurant's reputation depends very much on its food. The money you pay the chef might be one of your best investments in the restaurant.

The manager's role in food quality

The chef's domain is the kitchen and the food. Many restaurant managers are intimidated by chefs, because chefs have expertise in the field that gives definition to what the restaurant is: a place you can buy food that can be readily eaten. Since the manager is the person ultimately in charge of the whole operation, however, he must have a defined role in the functional aspects of the kitchen. He certainly has the right to walk in and make observations. His job is to coordinate all jobs to service the customer effectively. He must get along with the chef and at the same time look out for the other aspects of the restaurant.

In a smaller restaurant it is a good idea for a manager to learn some of the cooking techniques used in the restaurant, one never knows when a temperamental chef will walk out without notice. This can be an embarrassment to establishments with a limited staff. By learning some of the cooking involved, a manager insures the consistency that every restaurant needs. In a smaller restaurant, learning some of the basic cooking is not that difficult and knowing how to assemble the dishes certainly can come in handy.

The prime task of a manager should be as a motivator and clarifier. The manager should be someone who can promote the needs of the customers and wait staff to the kitchen employees. He has to inspire the kitchen staff to recognize how important customers really are. I used to say things in the kitchen like: "Don't serve anything you wouldn't eat yourself." "You would want your steak cooked to your taste. Cook it to their preference!" "You wouldn't want a soggy salad!" In most restaurants there is a physical barrier between cooks and customers. They seldom see each other. The manager must periodically remind the kitchen staff of the importance of the customer.

A manager is sometimes a mediator between kitchen staff and service people. When this role is warranted, he or she must immediately become an advocate for the customer. Mention of the customer usually settles all disputes quickly. A manager's prime concern must be the customer, but at the same time he must strike a delicate balance between *all* parties—service staff, cooks, and customers.

GOOD SERVICE

There are important roles for supervisors in assuring good service. Poor floor management is easily detectable in any restaurant. The wait staff is unhappy and customers are irritated. If unhappy customers told us what caused their dissatisfaction, their complaints might include:

1. waiting too long to be seated when there were tables available

2. waiting too long for the food

3. constantly being ignored when trying to get service, and

4. unfriendly service.

Some waitresses and waiters can leave you unhappy even though they are technically good wait staff. We had a waitress whose skills were nothing exceptional—on par with the rest of our wait staff. But from a good will point of view and from a sales point of view, she was the best. Regardless of what happened during her shift, she presented herself in such a way that customers not only liked her, they loved her. She might have forgotten to bring a drink to a table, but when people left the establishment you could always see them waving with big smiles saying, "Good night, Mary" or "Bye, Mary" or "We'll see you, Mary." They might have been steadies or new customers, it didn't matter. Customers enjoyed themselves at the restaurant, and Mary had a lot to do with it. She had all of the personality traits that likeable people have. She was friendly, kind, humble, and she always tried hard.

Not everyone has these desirable characteristics, but it is important that an establishment be known as a friendly place to go. The manager or owner himself should occasionally mingle with the customers. It is not necessary to get into long conversations. Simple greetings and verbal niceties are sufficient. Most people are honored by the fact that they were greeted by the big boss.

The host, hostess, waiters, and waitresses are the restaurant's ambassadors of good will. They should think of themselves as being on stage. They are the nice girls and great guys in a Broadway production; it follows that they should never have their backs to the audience! When customers are irritated by lack of service and see waiters and waitresses engrossed in their own secrets, ignoring them, the irritation turns to anger. It is disconcerting to most people when service personnel are nestled together, whispering. The staff's responsibility is to make the customers as comfortable as possible.

When something goes wrong, the restaurant's stance should be one of humility. Most customers are nice and are going to be more forgiving toward a humble wait person. We tell our new waitresses to be up-front with patrons before they take an order: "Hello, my name is Jean. This is my first day. I hope I can do a good job for you." This will generally bring compassion and understanding from people. Everyone can relate to having a first day doing something. On the other hand, let's assume that Jean says nothing and goofs up the order. There is a good chance the customers will be dissatisfied. By this time it is too late for Jean to say she is a new waitress.

The manager must constantly remind the wait staff of the importance of the customer. He or she must tell the staff that the customers have made an effort to honor the establishment with their presence. They have showered, shaved, dressed, driven or walked, and given this night of their lives to our place and our presence. In return, the staff must make a maximum effort to make sure they have an enjoyable stay.

An awareness that the customers didn't just walk in, but made a choice to be here, is an all-too-elusive concept in most restaurants. Usually people are not in a full-service restaurant because of convenience. They can go to another establishment just as readily as they came here. (Bad service will be the catalyst that inspires them to do that.) People go out to eat because they want satisfaction and joy; they want to feel like king and queen for the night; they want to be served and treated well. And if they pay the bill, they deserve all of it.

It is up to the front line people, the host, hostess, and wait staff, to foster friendly interactions. Every day for thirty years, I would say to my staff, "We are the friendliest restaurant around!" It was my duty to spread this attitude to the staff. Management must constantly remind staff to use appropriate greetings and farewells, and must also monitor the employees interactions with customers. Friendliness must be pervasive in a restaurant.

Handling complaints and the unexpected

Hostesses should be trained to assist wait staff and handle minor complaints. Good hostesses can often turn bad situations around and make the restaurant look good in the eyes of customers.

A supervisor, too must be effective in dealing with the unexpected. There will always be those who are disruptive after a couple of drinks. If there is an embarrassing situation, the goal should be to defuse the situation; or, if things get unruly, to have a contingency plan, such as calling the police or other security people. The main concern should be for the comfort of the rest of the customers.

We once had a gentleman in our dining room who was having a heart attack. A large woman about three tables away immediately began performing the Heimlich maneuver on the poor man, a technique used to help someone who is choking. When I got to the table, I heard the man's ribs cracking from the force of her arms. He was moaning in a very low, chest voice, so I quickly realized that this customer was *not* choking to death. This woman was well intentioned, but unrelenting! I had the waitress call the paramedics immediately and I eventually convinced the overzealous lady that the man's breathing apparatus was functioning and that he might have a different problem.

The ambulance arrived and the medics handled everything professionally. After a couple of days in the hospital the man's heart was okay, but his ribs were still sore.

People encounters are the name of the game in the restaurant business. If people feel good about themselves while in a facility, their return to it is almost guaranteed.

GOOD ATMOSPHERE

What do people do in restaurants? They sit. They socialize. They eat! There doesn't seem to be any great mystery in providing the space to do these things. However, humankind frequently provides a special space where people can sit, socialize, and eat simultaneously. In most western cultures that place is called the dining room.

In Williamsburg, Virginia, one can visit the dining room in the Governor's House; at Monticello, there is a beautiful dining room that Thomas Jefferson designed. In television documentaries, I have noticed that the dining rooms of the famous and infamous are very special places in their homes. In Michelangelo's Last Supper, the dining area is heavenly. Americans have designed their dining rooms as composites of traditional styles that date back several thousand years.

Two themes that seem to be prevalent in western eating environments are warmth and comfort. These are relative concepts, but restaurant atmosphere cannot be measured by scientific formulas. The reason I mention warmth and comfort is that whenever I ask people what they like about a place, one of the things they mention most is atmosphere. When I ask, "What about the atmosphere?" most answers have to do with warmth and comfort. Movie and television sets depicting dining rooms point toward warm and comfortable environments. Why would people want to dine in a room that has a giant orange globe affixed above their heads? There are prospective owners who are always looking for outlandish gimmicks in room design that they think will attract customers. However, it doesn't appear that what makes dining a pleasurable experience has changed that much over the years.

History tells me that if I were to build a dining room, I should look to traditional examples of excellence. They seem to be more related to time-tested human wants and needs than to fadism. If it ain't broke, don't fix it.

Prime consideration must be given to making the decor fit the theme of the restaurant. For example, traditional meat and seafood establishments could have colonial, Tudor, or contemporary styles, but should not have Roman fountains or gondolas, which would be more suitable in an Italian restaurant. If possible, the theme of the decor should begin at the front door and continue throughout the various rooms, even into the restrooms. A clever decorator can establish a theme in an effective and inexpensive manner. I know of an owner who spent very little money on some decorative goods that were old, but not genuine antiques. He built a few shelves around his dining room for the display of these "antiques." He followed up by having his waitresses wear black skirts and white blouses. Three cans of texture paint later, he had a colonial restaurant. (Bear in mind that it is important for waitresses and waiters to dress according to decor.)

Cleanliness in the dining area, the entry ways, and the restrooms is a big word-of-mouth consideration. These are the kinds of things restaurant patrons talk about when describing a facility. The most desired comments are: "The foods was great!" "The service was great!" "The atmosphere was great!" "The place was nice and clean!"

CONSISTENT HOURS

Once there was a restaurant that did a respectable six-nights-a-week business until someone came up with an idea for Tuesday nights. The management decided to close the kitchen and the restaurant to dinner patrons on Tuesday and advertise dancing to a rock band. The new policy seemed to be a success: the rock band had a good draw and the establishment made a nice initial profit. But it turned out to be a very bad business policy.

First of all, it angered the steady Tuesday night dinner patrons. The manager forgot to consider that the people he angered most by his policy change were the real fans of the restaurant; they were out supporting it on Tuesday nights. Greed made him forget what made his restaurant a success: food, service, and consistency.

In bringing in a rock group he also lost his strong identity as a restaurant. This identification took time to build up, but eroded quickly. The Tuesday night crowds dwindled; the manager tried to promote dancing on a weekend night. He was gradually losing the fine restaurant concept. Within two years he was out of business. This place had been in business for thirty-five years, but it went down the tubes due to inconsistent scheduling.

When it is slow at the beginning of the week, waitresses have more time to cater to the needs of their customers; let them. Customers who are out dining on a Monday or Tuesday usually eat out frequently. A slow time is a good opportunity for the staff to put a little extra into the servicing effort. Their happy customers will promote by word of mouth.

I don't believe that restaurants should disrupt their normally scheduled hours for special events. Super Bowl, hockey, World Series, or basketball championship celebrations should be left to the sports bars.

An establishment must be open on a consistent and dependable basis. I know a manager who decided to close Mondays. After about two months and comments from some of the steady customers he decided to reopen on Mondays. This time business was slower than it was before. A month later he decided once again to close on Mondays. This inconsistent policy confused his patrons and, even worse, seemed to have a negative effect on business at the beginning and middle of the week. A customer should not be confused about when a restaurant might be open or closed. Successful restaurants have consistency both in food and scheduled serving hours.

SANITATION

The relationship between good sanitation and good will should be obvious, but it is often a neglected factor.

A well-known restaurant chain had an outlet in the northeast in which many patrons got sick after being exposed to salmonella bacteria. This bacteria is often carried by poultry, but is undetectable by smell or sight. It can be carried by utensils or hands, thereby contaminating other foods. Of course, if a number of people have to go to a hospital, and if the analysis by experts traces the source of the problem to a particular restaurant, the bad news will spread quickly. As a result of such notoriety, the restaurant closed and has never reopened.

If a restaurant is shut down by health inspectors due to unsanitary kitchen practices, the reputation of the establishment can be severely damaged. Cleanliness of all kitchen areas, including counter surfaces, equipment, and utensils is essential in preventing bacteria growth and insect infestation. Refrigeration must constantly be monitored so that correct temperatures are maintained. All storage areas must be kept clean to avoid food contamination. Kitchen staff must learn to properly thaw frozen foods and properly refrigerate hot foods.

Of course, a manager must insist on good personal hygiene from all employees.

1. No one should be allowed to smoke while on duty.

2. Every person who carries food or drink must have proper hair restraints.

3. Every employee must be and look clean—clean clothes, fingernails, hands, aprons, etc.

Sanitation is an important ingredient of good will. There is nothing more disgusting than being in a restaurant and noticing an employee who looks grimy. Most diners who see this hope that the person had nothing to do with the preparation of their food.

4

PERSONNEL MANAGEMENT

4

PERSONNEL MANAGEMENT

THE SUCCESS OF ANY BUSINESS USUALLY PARALLELS THE PRODUC-
tivity of its personnel. While many things influence productivity, personnel
management is the most important. It is management that directs and has the
greatest impact on the activities of the work force.

The importance of management is known to stock-market traders. Changes
in CEOs usually have a dramatic impact on the trading price of a stock. Top
management people in large corporations are the leaders who influence production, sales, and new-product development. They must be respected by their subordinates to be effective.

MANAGEMENT STRUCTURE

The pyramid

Every human organization has a chain of command. There are those who make
policy, and there are those who make sure that the policies are carried out.
Generally, the larger the organization, the greater the number of people clustered
near the top. To foster singularity of purpose and avoid chaos, the chain of command must have a specific structure. The ideal composition usually has one chief
administrator, who has a few subordinates, who have a few subordinates, who
have a few subordinates, and so on, and so on. The charts that show this organizational structure are generally drawn in the form of a pyramid. In a large

manufacturing corporation, the chart should show the CEO on top (with a spot for the board of directors), then the various senior vice presidents, then the assistant vice presidents, underneath them the middle managers, and toward the bottom, the workforce.

The western world has used the pyramid extensively to show the relationships between people, between people and the environment, and between people and other forms of life. In the charts that I've seen, humans are always in the top block of the pyramid, showing their superiority. Of course it is always humans who draw these charts from their point of view. If a lion could draw, we might have an entirely different-looking chart.

The idea of being on top of the pyramid symbolizes success in western cultures. Higher means better. For example, we talk about climbing the ladder of success. In sports, one team finishes at the top of the division. When a person is not getting through to his or her boss, he or she is told, "You shouldn't go over his head." When a corporal becomes a sergeant he or she moves up in rank. A good student wants to be at the top of the class. A corporate vice president is high up in the organization. In the recording "New York, New York," Frank Sinatra sings of being on top of the heap.

Hospitality houses such as restaurants also have organizational structures that have a general manager or manager at the top of the chain of command.

A creative manager, however, might be able to draw a structure that is different from the pyramid to illustrate the chain of command. He could draw a graph with the potential for continuous movement, one which has the whole staff in positions that allow for cross currents of communication. In such a scheme, the dishwasher has a feeling of dignity, rather than a feeling of being crushed at the bottom of the pyramid.

In large organizations, it is difficult for someone close to the bottom (who might have a very creative idea) to penetrate the layers of management above and get his idea to the right person. A small business needs every staff member working in concert with every other to adequately service the public. The manager must make every effort to maximize communication between bosses and workers. Waitresses must not only communicate with waitresses, they must communicate with the entire staff. Teamwork is essential to the success of a restaurant. (See Fig. 6)

The family restaurant

Family enterprises are a curious phenomenon in the food-service industry. They seem to be either hugely successful or complete failures.

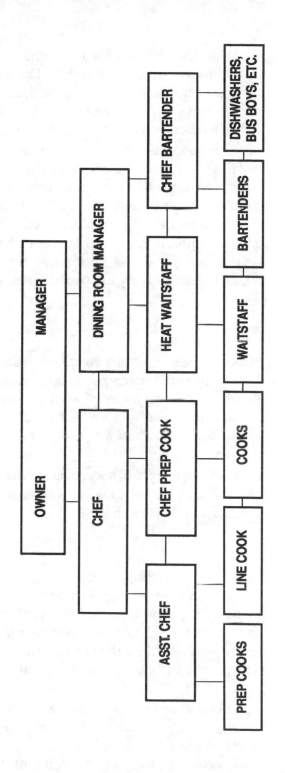

FIGURE 6

The problems may begin when the father, sons, mother, and daughters are all adults in one common business enterprise. Who should be the CEO? If it is the father, then the son, who may be the head of his household, must become a subordinate. This may lead to problems. The restaurant suddenly mimics the original household of father, mother, and children.

When the family structure becomes the most important element of a restaurant it has little chance of success. On the other hand, if families (whose members by nature almost always want the best for one another and love each other) understand that it is not family dynamics but rather business dynamics that make a restaurant a success, their establishments can succeed. Democracy must prevail and the family must assemble a structure of shared responsibility. It is important that they elect a titular head, or a moderator, so meetings will go smoothly. Family unity, after all, and business unity are two different phenomena. (See Figs. 7 and 8)

Leadership

The word leadership evokes images of Caesar conquering Gaul or Washington crossing the Delaware and leading his troops to victory. The leader is the boss, the guy calling the shots and telling everyone else what to do. In sports, the athlete running around whacking his teammates on the back is sometimes referred to as the emotional leader of the team. There are many ways that one can show leadership.

Let's look at the kinds of leadership that sociologists write about, and try to put them in a restaurant context. There are three kinds of leadership that I know of: charismatic, democratic, and authoritarian.

Charismatic leadership

The charismatic leader is successful in gaining followers because he or she is admired and adored due to his or her personal appeal; certain deeds he or she performed seem extraordinary. Some people have charisma to a limited degree. Like beauty, charisma is in the eyes of the beholder. In a restaurant, if a great number of the staff are working effectively because they admire the manager, he or she has charisma. However, it's rare to find charismatic leaders hanging around kitchens.

Charisma is a trait that one either has or doesn't have. It is not something that can be learned. It's like perfect pitch in music (a rare phenomenon where musicians know the exact sound of a note without hearing it). Perfect pitch is good to have, but one can become a great musician without it. Likewise, a res-

WHO IS THE BOSS IN THE RESTAURANT?

```
                        OWNER
                          |
        +-----------------+-----------------+
        |                                   |
   GENERAL MANAGER                    PERSONNEL MANAGER
        |                                   |
   +----+-----------+              +--------+---------+
   |                |              |                  |
FOOD BEVERAGE   CONTROLLER    ASST. CHEF        BUILDING ENG.
  MANAGER           |              |                  |
   |                |              |                  |
EXECUTIVE        COOKS         DISHWASHER         HOSTESS          GROUNDS
  CHEF                                                            PERSONNEL
   |
BARTENDER

WAITSTAFF
```

FIGURE 7

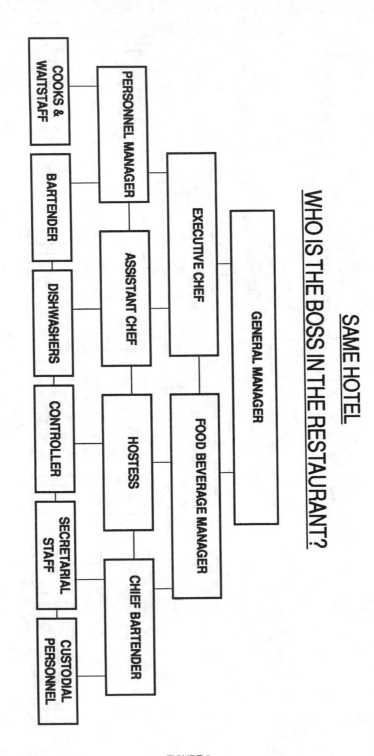

WHO IS THE BOSS IN THE RESTAURANT?

SAME HOTEL

FIGURE 8

taurant manager can become an effective leader without having a charismatic personality.

Democratic leadership

The democratic leader learns how to share authority and responsibility. He or she tries to get everyone to participate in the discussions about the needs of the establishment. He or she motivates by encouraging the staff to be creative, contribute new ideas, and come forth with criticisms. He or she demonstrates that the main goal is to motivate people to meet the ultimate objective—a well-run restaurant—and not to gain power over them.

The democratic leader is apt to gain knowledge from the opinions of the staff. If he is good he will get ideas from part-time workers, such as dishwashers and bus boys. They can be knowledgeable about specific aspects of the restaurant. If workers are not afraid to talk to the boss, the boss can gain a wealth of information from them. The democratic leader is usually effective at delegating authority to other democratic leaders, and, just as important, knowing which staff members *shouldn't* be given too much authority.

I once worked with a woman who was brilliant in many ways, but was not exactly loaded with tact and compassion. She was not a "people person." She worked in the office, did the books, made deposits, took inventory, and had other duties that kept her from having authority over any workers. Among her duties was responsibility for the first-aid kit. Upon returning to work after a vacation, she noticed that the kit was out of band-aids. She was walking toward the office when suddenly one of the prep cooks badly cut himself. Her reaction was unbelievable! She ran up to him screaming, "Did you have to cut yourself? We're all out of band-aids?"

The response, of course, was not exactly appropriate to the situation. She was yelling at a man whose prime concern was the date of his last tetanus shot. Her response assumed that workers should check the first-aid kit before beginning work; if it's well stocked, they can go right ahead and have a blood bath. The moral is, be very careful when delegating any kind of authority. A little power in the hands of the wrong person can have a devastating impact on the morale of your staff.

Authoritarian leadership

Unfortunately, the authoritarian leader is found in many restaurants. He has the first and last word on the activities of the workers. He usually does not take kindly to advice and tends to be a threatening person who uses fear as a motivational device. He does not understand that morale is an important ingredient of productivity. He has difficulty delegating authority, therefore little is done without his participation.

The authoritarian leader has usually gained enemies within the workforce. This is hardly a healthy environment in a restaurant, which depends so heavily on good public relations. The staff turnover rate is very high in a food-service establishment that has an autocratic manager; the danger is that, with a constantly changing work staff, it is difficult for a restaurant to attain a high degree of consistency. (I also believe that it is difficult for an authoritarian boss to gain any real respect.)

Respect

I get confused when people talk about likability and respect as if they are totally opposite and mutually exclusive concepts. I've heard such things from managers as, "I'm not in a popularity contest; I don't care if nobody likes me, all I want is their respect." This kind of person usually ends up with nobody left in the place to respect him. Many people confuse respect with intimidation. I have heard, "I hated the guy, but I respected him!" My response is simple: "Why aren't you still working for him?"

I remember a general manager who scolded me because I allowed the employees to address me by my first name. She said, "I never allow anyone to call me by my first name. I insist they call me Mrs. Freeman." I felt like saying, "I guess you haven't been in the employee lunchroom lately."

The appearance of respect and actual respect are not necessarily the same. One cannot mandate a person's respect, but one can be liked and respected at the same time. The best manager is one who is both liked and respected by his employees.

So the conclusion is that a democratic leader who is both liked and respected is probably the best restaurant manager. It is also nice if this person has charisma, but, as mentioned above, it is not necessary.

Gaining respect through knowledge

Let's talk about the functions of this perfect manager and trace his relationship with the employees in the various departments of the restaurant. We know that the manager must have the respect of the employees. In order to gain respect the manager must demonstrate that he has skills, awareness, and knowledge of the workings of the whole establishment. The manager must show that he knows what's going on.

A good way to learn about the restaurant is to arrive at the facility at least an hour before anyone on the shift. The early-bird manager can spend time taking a quick visual inventory of the stock and observe the general condition of each area. By being two steps ahead in anticipating some of the problems, the manager will be better prepared to react in an effective manner.

A good manager should have a thorough knowledge of the financial status of the restaurant. This is important in employee relationships because one can give appropriate responses to questions about pay raises or the financial condition of the operation.

In the kitchen, the manager should understand the function of each job. He should also be aware of who is responsible for specific duties. If the manager has a particular skill, he or she should demonstrate a willingness to dig in and help occasionally. A demonstrated knowledge of the workings of kitchen equipment, for instance, will result in respect from the cooking staff. The more the manager knows, the more he will be respected.

Likewise, the manager should understand the duties of all serving personnel. Awareness of what is going on in the dining areas is essential for a manager. If he wants to inspire good service, the manager has got to be able to recognize what it consists of. The manager must also be able to recognize *bad* service so he can rectify it. The manager should know the precise job of the hostess or maitre d'. He should learn the exact perimeters of waitress sections so that he knows who to talk to if there is a problem.

Finally, the manager must know enough to be visible and available at the peak hours of business. A manager who is not there at the right time will not be respected. The manager who is knowledgeable will be better prepared to solve problems and gain the respect of the employees.

MANAGER-EMPLOYEE RELATIONS

"She is very tactful." "He is considerate." "She's diplomatic." "He shows sensitivity." All of the statements describe someone who is likeable. These traits, which are desirable assets for a good restaurant manager, are usually manifested through communication. Mannerisms, tone of voice, and good choice of words result in a favorable impression. A restaurant manager who is a skillful communicator can produce a feeling of high morale among the staff.

I remember a kitchen manager who changed jobs at least twice a year. Whenever he was asked by a subordinate why anything had to be done in a certain way, he would snap, "Because I know something that you don't know. Just do it!" This is not the attitude that motivates employees. Workers should have the right to ask questions about things that concern them. A manager should handle answers diplomatically and tactfully.

Good communication

To be respected, the manager must set the environment for employees and management to have mutual respect. When asking an employee to do something, clarity is important. Consider this request: "Will you go into the freezer and get some ribs?" From this an employee cannot discern the kind and number. "Will you go into the freezer and take out two boneless ribs?" is much clearer. It is always good to clarify the reason for a particular task. How would you feel if someone walked up to you and asked, "Will you take the ladder out and climb on to the roof and wait until I tell you what to do next?" This type of request is belittling to a worker. A much better approach might be, "We are going to replace the light bulbs on the security fixtures. Will you take a ladder and climb onto the roof? I'll hand you the lights one at a time." This explains the project and how it is to be done. The former request implies that the employee cannot handle more than one concept at a time.

Unclear communications during busy hours can lead to many costly mistakes by both cooks and servers. Most workers who know the chain of command do not have to be ordered around as if they were in the military. When a supervisor's main task is to motivate and inspire employees, it is not necessary to give instructions in the form of a demand. "John, go down and get a bag of salt!" could be, "John, can you go down and get us a bag of salt?" In this way the directive becomes a request. A slight change in the manner and wording of the directive makes the subordinate a little more comfortable, and you get the same results.

A manager must know the staff. Some are very sensitive people who will almost fall apart if they are reprimanded. A manager must be very careful in his or her choice of words. A reprimand must be made with consideration for the facts and never on instinct. When a manager does not know exactly who is guilty he must never make accusations.

1. *Right.* "Who left the freezer door open?"

2. *Wrong.* "Joe, why did you leave the freezer door open?"

A reprimand must always be a *private* encounter between manager and employee. Employees should never be scolded in front of fellow workers, customers, or anyone else.

Kitchen frivolity

Jokes and kidding are part of most work situations. People can talk with each other and work at the same time. For much of the day, a restaurant kitchen is just such a place. There is always kidding, people zinging each other with "derogatory" remarks, all in fun. These are generally healthy interactions because they help break the boredom of repetitive work. Remember that some people can be sensitive, though one must be careful with this type of kidding.

For a short time, I worked as a line cook in a kitchen that had the usual 2½ foot aisle space for quick, efficient cooking. I was supervising a woman in her early twenties, about 5 feet 6 inches, and weighing at least 250 pounds. When I worked with her in that aisle, it was like being in the biggest pillow fight of my life, and I was always losing. I couldn't move without her bumping me. She was always talking about herself and food, but in such a way that one wondered whether she knew that she was fat. I remember her saying, "I don't eat anything all day, the only time I eat is at night." So there I was thinking to myself, "Well what do you do, then, go out into the field and devour the neighbor's cow?" Another time she said, "For a long time all I ate was cornflakes." The zinger was, "I remember. That was the time Kelloggs's stock tripled in price." I would think of those digs, but I would *never* vocalize them. Sometimes, I would have to leave and break into a fit of laughter in the restroom. Don Rickles would have had a ball with this woman, because she always left herself wide open for a dig. I didn't dare say anything. I was her supervisor; besides, she was a lot bigger than I was.

Discrimination

A few years ago "honey," "sweetheart," and "darling" were words used quite freely in a restaurant setting. Today, a manager can get into trouble for using any one of these terms with a member of the opposite sex.

A manager cannot use gestures or words that might be construed as sexual harassment. If a manager consistently calls a woman "honey" he may be creating problems for himself that he is not aware of. Let's assume that a woman works very well at a particular job. The manager begins calling her "honey," as a well-intentioned gesture with nothing else intended. He just appreciates her work and this is his way of showing it. Suddenly her work habits deteriorate and he is constantly meeting with her to reprimand her for the poor quality of her work. Six weeks later, with no improvement in sight, he fires her. She could bring him to court for sexual harassment and stand a good chance of winning.

I have always felt that the real obscenities in the American language are racial slurs. Restaurants are places where there is a chance for great social interaction. Bigotry and discriminatory remarks, like sexual harassment, simply have no place in a restaurant environment.

Compliments

Compliments can be doled out in ways that are counterproductive. I once had a manager who was constantly telling people what a good job they were doing. It was sickening: an employee couldn't cut up an onion without hearing "good job." In such an atmosphere, when someone really does a good job, it is barely recognizable. There should be a minimum standard of behavior; if someone exceeds the minimum, only then should a compliment be given.

The opposite of this is the boss who never gives compliments for anything. When someone says, "Wow, Sally did a great job on the specials," he replies, "So what? She's getting paid for it, isn't she?" When an employee tries extremely hard and has accomplished something that is beneficial to the establishment, the work should be praised.

The boss who motivates

Emotional extremes on the manager's part can be disruptive and undermine productivity. I like descriptions from personnel that the boss is firm but fair. They know exactly the dimensions of behavior that the manager will tolerate. They know the manager and understand the limitations. Such managers are corrective in an educative manner, rather than being overly patronizing. When both managers and workers know each other well enough, productive interaction can result. When the workers constantly say things like, "I really don't know how to take that guy," I know right away the working atmosphere is unhealthy.

A good restaurant supervisor will get in the habit of using key words and key phrases. In the dining room, a manager can give constant reminders to the wait staff—"be friendly," "smile pretty," "make everything right." Successful coaches in sports use this approach all the time. The phrases become redundant cliches, but they are not meant to be revelations, they are meant to inspire performance. I would say things like, "You've got a great smile, use it on the customer!" Or, "Hey, look! All the nicest people are sitting in our dining room, and all of the greatest people in the world are waiting on them." In the kitchen I would say, "There are a whole bunch of people who love your food out there." I call these phrases spirit builders!

Inspire efficiency

Waste is a big problem in many restaurant kitchens. It must be kept to a minimum, otherwise it can greatly reduce one's profit. Product is paid for by the ounce, and a manager must always demonstrate his concern for its preservation at that same ounce-by-ounce level. If carelessness is the rule in a moderately-sized restaurant kitchen, the cost of waste can amount to thousands of dollars per year. With this in mind I constantly say, "Remember, food is gold."

Staff morale

An organization is not required to guarantee happiness to its workers; however, neither is it supposed to create an environment in which people are always miserable. Very often the manager's reply to reports of low staff morale is, "We're not here to make them happy. We're here to run a restaurant!" This is true, but when morale is very low, the management is doing something that is making the staff unhappy (or failing to do something that would make them happy). Maintaining morale is management's responsibility.

Standards for communication

Create a wholesome working environment where people feel accepted. There are certain kinds of treatment that are repulsive to all human beings. When people want to be heard—whether it is a grievance or a creative idea—they don't want their voices to fall on deaf ears. Of course, there are the constant complainers. But when a manager shuts his ears to all those who feel that they have something to say, he begins to fail as a manager.

The person who has an idea for *anything* that affects the restaurant should be listened to and encouraged to come up with more suggestions. Unfortunately, many managers stunt the creative growth of their personnel. Listen to everyone! I've received many good ideas from young dishwashers. *Every employee has the potential for inventive ideas.*

Rumors

Rumors, especially those that are not true, can be detrimental to an establishment. "The restaurant is for sale!" "The chef is quitting!" "They are going to fire Sally!" All gossip! Who cares? The manager should care. These are exactly the kinds of rumors that affect morale.

Everyone remembers the game where someone whispers something into someone's ear; it is passed on this way until it gets to the last person, who vocalizes it to the group. Invariably, what the last person says has little or no resemblance to the original phrase. This is exactly how rumors spread, without a definite form and left open to interpretation. Usually they begin with a small incident and turn into an exaggerated story. But, a highly accessible manager who is easy to communicate with can stop an ugly rumor dead in its tracks.

"We hear the place is up for sale!" This is one of the most difficult rumors for a restaurant owner to deal with. If it is not handled properly it can lead to a lot of instability and insecurity among the employees. If the restaurant is not for sale, the manager must try to stop the rumors immediately. This may be done by approaching individuals or groups quickly, and making an unqualified denial. If the rumor is very strong, the manager should call an emergency meeting and very quickly put the concerns to rest.

If management *is* negotiating to sell, and there is a lot of hearsay about it, the manager must take a very cautious approach. Many restaurant sales are never consummated, and management is often left with a staff that will have doubts about its future. I have never been faced with this situation, but I *have* advised other managers whose restaurants were on the selling block. First, use the cliche, "Everything in this world is for sale for the right price"; second, "If this place is sold you will be the first to know." The staff needs the trust and reassurances that only management can offer.

The rumor that someone might be fired is one that can be unpleasant for the whole staff. The management must try to avoid this problem with forthrightness. Gossip is embarrassing and threatening to both the establishment and personnel, but a manager who communicates well can stop rumors effectively.

Understanding the abilities of the staff

Assignments and responsibilities must relate to the talents of the individuals. Some workers are faster than others. Some are meticulous and work toward perfection. Some are people-oriented; others are technically and mechanically inclined.

I was in a home-improvement store recently, and as I walked by a giant stack of bags of cement mix, I noticed that they were about to tumble. I took two bags of lime and threw them up on top, hoping to create some balance in the stack, so I could warn the manager. This was a potentially dangerous situation.

My maneuver did not work. The stack tumbled and one of the bags opened, covering me from head to toe. I dusted myself off as best I could, but I still must have looked like I was in a flour mill when an earthquake hit. The stacks behind me started to wobble, so I left to get some help.

As I walked down an aisle, I noticed a clerk coming toward me, so naturally I assumed that he would inquire about what had happened. I figured that there couldn't be too many people walking around town who looked like an Italian Frosty the Snowman! I tried to voice my concerns, but he just walked by me as if I were invisible. I chased after him, telling him what had happened, but still no response. Finally, tearing mad, I stepped in front of him. For the fourth time I loudly proclaimed what had happened. He finally looked me in the eye and said, "Look buddy, I heard you the first time!"

I left the store extremely agitated. I called the manager from home, told him what had happened, and said that I thought the clerk's behavior was disgraceful. He answered that he was sorry about what had happened, but then he began to defend his employee. He said, "Roland is very bad with the public, but he knows more about lumber and materials than anyone!"

Here was a case where Roland was not the problem; management was to blame. Roland should never have been out on the floor waiting on customers with a tag on his chest that read "CLERK." He should have been given a job that he was better suited for, one that didn't require interaction with customers.

If a manager knows the capabilities and the limitations of his staff, he or she will be better prepared to give proper work assignments. The faster line cooks can be given certain duties and the slower ones assigned to others, each according to their talents. When a person is doing a job that he can do well, his performance and well being results in the best possible situation for both employer and employee.

Delegating authority

We all know of the supervisor who got to that position by hard work and firsthand knowledge of almost every job in the establishment. Sometimes, though, as managers, these people have problems delegating authority. When something goes wrong they try to do it all themselves. Managers must learn the art of teaching. A good teacher does not perform the student's work, but rather leads him and shows him how to do it.

In a restaurant, there are too many things going on for any one person to keep track of them all. There must be people other than the manager who are responsible for the completion of duties. Responsibility for purchasing, for example, should be given to the person who has the skills applicable to buying. That may not be the restaurant manager.

The person who is put into a supervisory position must be able to get along with people. Management potential is also a prerequisite. The manager has to develop the inclination to delegate authority to the appropriate individuals. Telling people that they have a particular role to play can be quite tricky. Authority can be interpreted differently depending on a person's background.

Recently, many Americans have been trying to emulate Japanese management techniques. Firms have hired Japanese supervisors to train their managers or have sent people to Japan to study their management style. The reason for this is obvious: Japan's economy is booming and Japan has a very high productivity level. One of the elements in the Japanese philosophy is an intensive set of communication standards.

This is to be commended, because good interactions with people can lead to high levels of human accomplishment. I believe that we cannot incorporate all of the Japanese management styles into our systems, however, because of the many cultural differences that exist. For example, failure to the average Japanese person is shameful. While nobody wants to fail, shame resulting from failure is not a motivating factor in the United States. Can't you hear it now? "Hey Ralph, you'd better do a good job or it'll bring shame on you!" You don't hear American bosses telling their subordinates, "Do a good job so that you can avoid shame!" There are different motivational factors inherent in different cultures. Not all of "the Japanese way" can—or should—be taught to Americans.

SETTING POLICIES

Americans generally have a democratic notion of the distribution of authority. With this in mind, we can establish three criteria for good restaurant policy regarding employees.

1. Restaurant policy must be within the guidelines of federal, state, and local labor laws.

2. Restaurant policy must be made known to all employees.

3. Restaurant policy must be mutually beneficial.

Labor laws

The United States Department of Labor, the relevant state organizations, and local board, and police departments can be sources for understanding the labor laws. These regulations must be adhered to by all employers. They regulate minimum wage, equipment use, maximum hours before a break, the minimum time allotted per break, child labor laws, job classifications, specific limits of job definitions, minimum hours to be compensated per day, what defines uniform, what is hazardous, illegal discrimination, alien hiring, job compensation insurance, and health insurance.

It is an awesome task to learn all these rules. The laws were passed as a reaction to unfair business practices in the past; their proponents were unions and legislators who wanted to improve conditions in the workplace. There are many more concerns that labor laws affect, and I am certainly not an expert at understanding all of them. However, I have one slogan when it comes to dealing with any government agency: "Meet with them before they meet with you!"

The labor agencies have pamphlets and other written materials that can be quite helpful to any personnel manager; read them. It is also a good idea to get to know the agents by name. Most representatives of labor law enforcement bodies can help before one formulates policy for employees; once a disgruntled employee files a complaint, it is too late.

If an initial conference with an agent shows the restaurant manager to be one who seeks to be in compliance with regulations, complaints may be handled in a less volatile manner. Do not make the mistake of seeing labor officials and agency representatives as adversaries. State agencies can help define what equipment should not be used by certain age groups. Police can help define who can and who cannot serve alcohol.

The basic rule is simple: know the agencies and be sure that restaurant policies adhere to the labor laws.

Salary, benefits, and staff morale

I have a recipe for employer-employee relations that I call the "steak-to-sizzle formula." In this recipe, the steak is the perceived quality of the job—reasonable pay and overall job satisfaction. On the other hand, the sizzle is the benefits—vacations, insurance, meal discounts, rewards, and bonuses. Most managers believe that if you improve the sizzle, the steak will look better and productivity will improve. When morale is low, a manager can often be heard saying, "What's the matter with these people? We give them everything they want!" "Everything" for most people means getting up in the morning with the knowledge that they are going to a job they enjoy.

I once worked for a nationally affiliated group of hotels. My office adjoined the restaurant: I could see morale deteriorating every day. Make no mistake: the company paid well and had terrific benefits for all employees. Second-level managers had free meals, free hotel privileges anywhere in the country, total health insurance bonuses, and so on. All this, and everyone was miserable.

My job was to help the staff and to formulate policy for one of their new hotels across the state line. While I was having lunch, the assistant manager asked me if there was any chance she could be transferred to the new outfit. I told her that the new hotel was going to have fewer benefits: "We're not giving out privilege cards, there will be a limited menu for the employees, and you'll have to pay fifty percent of the menu price." Her response: "I don't care, I just want to go to a job were I'm not miserable every day!" Sizzle does not necessarily render a good steak.

Too many benefits can actually result in a kind of regressive tax on the better employees. Let's assume that per capita benefits cost is $3.00. The funds allotted are shared equally by both good and less productive personnel. If benefits are minimized, the monies saved could be given out in the form of pay raises to the more productive employees, and each good employee might receive a raise that more then compensates for the $3.00 he lost!

Realistically, the greatest reward for any employee is to have a job where he is paid fairly and has positive feelings about the work. Management has the responsibility for creating a challenging, upbeat, and productive workplace.

Making policy known

During the initial job interview, a prospective employee is usually told the job description, the hours, the benefits, and name of the immediate superior. In many instances, workers only learn the rules and regulations piecemeal from other employees. Too often, it is a co-worker who must say something like, "You can't take your break in the dining room; you have to go to the employee lounge!"

A restaurant should have its policies printed and given to each worker at the beginning of employment. When a person walks into a new job, he or she is apprehensive. A new line cook might worry that his particular talents do not fit into the new environment. He might be concerned that the place could get packed and he wouldn't be able to handle it. He feels like the new kid on the block. Everyone understands the feeling of going to a new job; everyone has done it. There is so much to worry about! Make the "initiation" as easy as possible.

An employer can remove some of the insecurities by making the basic rules known in a clear manner. Large companies have employee handbooks in which they describe the company in glowing terms, map out the facility, and detail the rules and regulations. A small restaurant doesn't need an elaborate policy pamphlet; it can get by with a couple of pages listing the benefits and regulations. This should be given to every employee and posted on a bulletin board in an area noticeable to everyone. (The best place to post any announcement is close to the employee time clock. This is also a perfect place for the weekly schedules.)

What employees must know

Every new worker should be made aware that a predetermined period will be considered a training period. This gives a person a good idea of the progress that should be made daily. In addition, everyone should know who to contact in the event of absence. In many instances, the boss finds out too late that a person is not coming in: "Yes, I called in sick, I talked to Harold the dishwasher. He must have forgotten to tell you!"

Employees should be made aware of the dress code and of minimum standards of personal hygiene. There should be an explicit warning that anyone caught stealing will be promptly dismissed (and arrested)! They should know the length of time and the place for their breaks, and whether they should punch out during those breaks. There must be a policy regarding food discounts and what meals employees are allowed to order. Policies regarding vacations, paid holidays, and paid sick days should be posted, as well. There must be guidelines about scheduling days off and a prescribed method for obtaining replacements. Every employee must be made aware of the reasons for and methods of termination; if an employee is caught in a minor infraction, he/she should be given a written warning. (See Fig. 9.)

All major announcements, rules, and regulations must be posted.

Employee food policy

I am a strong opponent of free food for personnel. I don't know of one restaurant that feeds their help for free that makes a profit. Whenever anything is given away, it is lost. Employees take advantage of the privilege and get careless in both preparation and service. If it's free, they think, it can't be that important. I use the analogy of a household when explaining why food cannot be given away. If there are eighty employees, that is the equivalent of sixteen households (with five people in each house). So the natural question is, "Who can afford to buy groceries for the whole neighborhood?" Usually, people get the idea.

I believe in charging fifty percent of the menu price and limiting the meals to perhaps five easy-to-prepare items. One must remember the cooks are the people preparing all the food. They have their hands full cooking for the customers. Therefore a limited menu is fair and in the spirit of camaraderie. (See Fig. 10.)

Vinny's Restaurant

WARNING NOTICE

Date of Notice _____

This WARNING is being issued to

_____

For the following REASON: _____

_____

_____

_____

_____

_____

_____

_____

Employee's Signature_____

Manager's Signature _____

FIGURE 9

No. 2605

EMPLOYEE FOOD ORDER

NAME _____

DATE _____

_____

ORDER

_____

1/2 PRICE ON ALL ITEMS INCLUDING CANNED SODA AND MILK, EXCEPT 10% OFF ON
ALL STEAK AND SEAFOOD ENTREES. DISCOUNTS VALID WHILE WORKING ONLY.

_____

TO-GO ORDERS—ALL ITEMS 10% OFF

_____

AFTER RECEIVING ORDER, SUBMIT SLIP TO COUNTER CASHIER TO BE PUT IN
REGISTER & NOT RUNG UP.

_____

TOTAL COST $ _____

PAID_____UNPAID _____

CASHIER'S INITIALS_____

TO BE USED ONLY FOR FOOD ORDERS

FIGURE 10

5

PUBLIC RELATIONS
AND ADVERTISING

CREATING A POSITIVE IMAGE

THE PUBLIC IMAGE OF A RESTAURANT IS VITALLY IMPORTANT. IF IT is favorable, business will almost certainly increase. A manager, then, can be a promoter of good public relations if he has the skills to establish good will outside the restaurant's walls.

Building exterior

The exterior of a retail building is open to the scrutiny of both patrons and those who have never been inside the establishment. The grounds, parking area, flowers, shrubs, flags, statues, and signs are all part of the outside image of the restaurant; if the restaurant looks attractive on the outside there is an increased likelihood that new customers will enter the premises.

Some cosmetic improvements are not at all costly. I know of a gasoline station that plants flowers annually, resulting in a very attractive display. Once, I stopped and asked the owner, "Isn't it expensive to plant all those flats every spring?" He answered, "Yes, about $400; but a one-time newspaper ad is about the same price. The flowers give me good exposure for five whole months." This is a clever businessman!

Shrubs have a one-time cost, but can last as long as the building. A well-designed landscape can enhance the appearance of a restaurant on a year-round basis. A lined parking lot can add a feeling of organization and professionalism to an establishment.

If flags are to be a part of the exterior decor, be careful to include the American flag with proper lighting. If there are going to be other flags, the American flag must be highest. One must understand the surrounding community and be very careful when planning to use flags. Flags are generally symbols for groups of people, and of their ideas; a particular flag might anger a segment of a community.

Signs are extremely important

Signs tell in words who you are and what you do. To be effective, signs should be made by experts. A good looking sign can draw people's attention and build your customer base.

A sign must be set up properly and within the guidelines of the local and state authorities. The primary focus of a restaurant sign should be limited to the name of the restaurant: Michael's Restaurant; Michael's Food and Spirits; Michael's Food and Drink.

I recently drove to a consulting assignment where the sign had the name of the restaurant completely lost in the middle, surrounded by information about the lounge, food, 50s dancing, pool tables, and so on. I walked in and said to the owner, "You're not doing very good business, are you?" "No," he replied, "we're not doing well at all!" I said, "I can't even begin working for you until you change that sign; people aren't coming in because they're confused as to what you want them to come in for!"

Clarity and simplicity are very important for a restaurant sign, but that doesn't mean you are limited to only three or four words. If there is space, a portion of the sign can be used to promote daily dinner specials; lettering for the promotion part of the sign can be changed in just a few minutes. A restaurant can post a special for lunch and change the sign for the dinner specials very easily. The tracks and lettering for the promotion section can probably be purchased for less than $200. A "Specials" sign can be particularly effective on a heavily traveled road or highway. Once the sign and letters have been paid for, this becomes an effective form of free advertising.

Good citizenship

A restaurant always operates within a certain well-defined community, and its success can depend on how well it conforms to its surroundings. The sociological forces at work in every society are complex, however, good citizenship on the part of restaurants does not have to be complicated. Most community laws and established practices work for the common good. The closer a restaurant embraces the goals of community effort, the more it will enhance its potential for success.

Get along with officials. A restaurant manager must try to develop a cooperative relationship with city or town authorities. His licenses are signed by local officials, after all. The building inspector, board of health representative, fire inspector, and electrical inspector are usually only asking for compliance with the ordinances they are authorized to enforce. If one shows a willingness to cooperate and asks for clarification when certain bylaws are not completely understood, officials are, as a rule, more than willing to be helpful. An introductory call or visit to the local police by a restaurant manager can be helpful in establishing good will.

Most business people shy away from law enforcement authorities. This is a mistake! A manager should make the first move and introduce himself to the police department and state his restaurant's desire to become a good citizen of the community.

Community relations. The business community in your area can be quite effective in dealing with the greater community. Business groups can have input into the passage of laws and ordinances, many of which will affect restaurants. The groups are usually involved with popular charities, which can be good public relations. It is a good idea for a restaurant manager to get involved with the business organization in the area.

Most successful restaurant operators know and get along with their competition. It's a good practice. In one town I visited, the sign authority decided to do away with promotional outdoor advertising. This would have greatly affected ten restaurants. The owners all banded together, met with the licensing board, and came up with a compromise solution: promotional signs had to be attached to the permanent sign. The restaurant owners were satisfied, and the opponents of sign blight also walked away happy. This could not have been accomplished without camaraderie and unity among the restaurant owners.

Restaurant managers who get along can borrow products from each other, help each other with purchasing, and obtain necessary information that affects their industry. In one community, a group of friendly owners put together a common advertising effort that met with great success.

On the streets, a restaurant owner can and should be a well-known and visible person. Get in the habit of being friendly *outside* of the restaurant by greeting people at the local bank, post office, or other retail outlets within the geographical area. People usually feel honored when businesspeople in a community greet them, and this is a great way of fostering good will.

The media. Good public relations can also be fostered through the local newspapers. Large corporations, major sport teams, large institutions, and politicians call news conferences to get free publicity for themselves or their company. Why not take the same approach? To be sure, a restaurant owner can't call a news conference: none of the media would show up. Still, newspapers have spaces that have to be filled in every edition. They are always in need of little filler stories. A restaurant can help fill the void with tidbits like: "A New Chef," "New Interior Design," "Employee of the Month," "Restaurant Dishwasher Is Valedictorian." These are not stories that would get on the evening news broadcast, but if a manager fosters a good relationship with the local newspaper, there could be some favorable results. Some of these people like to be wined and dined; others refuse anything of the sort for the sake of editorial integrity. One should know the person in question well before offering to pay for a meal. (Be careful in this regard with all public figures. Most of them just want to be treated decently and with respect, not bribed.)

Community institutions. Support for local schools and colleges is always viewed with admiration by the citizens of a community. I believe a restaurant manager should always take time to introduce himself to the school administration, especially to the high school principal. Usually, a restaurant is heavily reliant on teenagers for part of its staff. Dishwasher, prep staff, bus boy, food runner, and salad maker: these are jobs that are suitable to people in their teens. Support for local youth sports teams, such as softball, Little League, soccer, hockey, and Pop Warner football can also put a restaurant in a favorable light.

Money for charitable causes should be part of the restaurant's advertising budget. Whenever possible, give gift certificates as well; sometimes they are more appreciated than money. When a gift certificate is auctioned at a charity raffle, it generally brings in more than its dollar value. It also has the potential for bringing in new customers!

So far we have talked about a great-looking building, and about a restaurant manager who is the best possible citizen in the community and has a flair for good public relations. All this is achieved with very little money—or no money at all in some instances. While you will want to get the most mileage possible out of your efforts at good citizenship, you will eventually also want to consider paid advertising as well.

ADVERTISING TECHNIQUES

Setting a direction

People who sell advertising usually approach prospective clients loaded down with pamphlets and literature documenting the effectiveness of their methods. Unfortunately, it takes a statistical expert to analyze much of the information in the brochures and to decide whether the data is applicable to a particular business.

Every restaurant owner would like to saturate the area with the restaurant's name. Although it's a good idea to put a high priority on positive restaurant exposure and visibility, one must always measure advertising in terms of cost effectiveness. Advertising space in a large newspaper that has a readership of 100,000 people can cost over $100 per column inch. A column inch ad, remember, is relatively small!

Before deciding on the type of advertising that is most desirable one must assess what the restaurant can afford and plan the advertising according to the budget. Once the budget has been determined, the target audience must be considered. Who are you trying to reach?

A restaurant should use a distinct and prominent logo in concert with its general theme in the visual advertising. The most inexpensive way to develop a logo is to search for a creative local artist, to tell him the theme of the facility, to commission him to draw three distinct logos, and to choose the most suitable one and have it printed.

The cost of having an advertising agency, by contrast, develop a logo can be outrageous.

Portrayal of a restaurant in whatever print medium chosen should include the theme of the establishment and the logo. An establishment should always market itself for what it really is in order to attract the appropriate clientele.

A restaurant manager who has a very strong feeling for conveying a particular theme can be a prime creative contributor to the advertising. The experts, such as advertising executives and newspaper specialists, can add the spunk, color, and imagination that will make an ad memorable.

What is a good ad? The most effective ads get right to the point, are not cluttered, and have a simple but memorable message.

In the late fifties, I knew a salesman who worked for a large typewriter firm. He would consistently outsell everyone in his company and sell more typewriters than any three other salesmen put together. I don't think this fellow ever went to high school. He didn't know how to type, and he knew very little about typewriters. However, he knew that his brand of typewriter had an automatic carriage return. That was all he needed. He refused schooling at company headquarters, where he could learn about other features of the equipment. His philosophy was to take a simple concept and market it to the hilt. He was an excellent example of the successful use of simplicity in selling.

The McDonald's Corporation has done an admirable job with its advertising. The words connected with restaurants should always be positive: goodness; joy; happiness; compassion; hope; friendliness; cleanliness; joviality. Through the years, McDonald's ads have been filled with these kinds of positive themes.

When I think of the concepts that work best in advertising for the food service industry, the word goodness leaps out at me immediately. "GOOD FOOD," "GOOD SERVICE," "GOOD VALUE," GOOD ATMOSPHERE." Any phrase, word, or visual idea that has a positive connotation should be considered a good direction for restaurant ads. Derogatory ads about the competition are tacky and inappropriate. There must be a projection of the idea that a restaurant's existence is based on excellence, and not that its existence and survival is due to the mediocrity of other establishments.

Kinds of ads

Advertising specials. When placing a value-oriented ad, a manager must be careful, and stay aware of what the competition is doing. For example, it would be embarrassing and ineffective to run an ad boasting a 16 oz. prime rib dinner for $10.95 when other restaurants using the same media are offering a 16 oz. prime rib dinner for $8.95. A manager must develop an instinct for value advertising by understanding the competition.

The effectiveness of value-oriented ads will be noticeable by the increase in business activity. "Crowds are at the door! It worked!"

The image ad, by contrast, can take a long time to be effective. It consists of low-key efforts at publicizing the theme, product, logo, and address of a business through the media over a long period. I call it "osmosis advertising." The idea is that a constant reminder will eventually lead to a popular and respectable image.

Loss leader. The loss leader advertising technique is generally used to stimulate new business and to get numbers of people into the facility. The leader is a product that is sold at or below cost to generate a great deal of traffic. I don't recommend the "all you can eat" promotion. I have not seen any real success in the places that have used this method. I tell my clients that the "all you can eat" crowd is the "all you can tolerate" crowd. Stay away from this gimmick.

Loss leaders can be effective if they are properly planned. There should be specific timetables for the first day and last day of the special. The staff must understand all of the aspects of the offer. The ad must be clear so the public understands precisely what they will be paying for. Of course, the strategy can backfire.

My father owned a restaurant that catered to college students; when school was not in session he would have a ninety percent drop in business. One summer he decided to remain open to see if he could gain some local and transient trade. He knew the marketing potential of the loss leader; he put a sign in the front window: "Hot Dogs—10¢ each."

I was working on the counter and my father was in the kitchen on a particularly slow afternoon when a neatly dressed gentleman came through the door and sat at the counter. He decided on a hot dog and a glass of beer. The frankfurter, he instructed me, had to be cut in half and then split into four pieces. He wanted it on two pieces of bread, toasted, with mayonnaise and chopped onions on one side, and on the other side, mustard and ketchup mixed together. The sandwich had to be cut in half diagonally.

I gave my father the order through a little window that looked into the kitchen. About 15 seconds later, I could hear his reaction. He must have used every swear word in both the Italian and English languages. He burned three pieces of toast while he was making the mustard and ketchup mixture. After about 15 minutes, he finally passed the sandwich through the window and whispered in my ear in a breathy, angry, heavy, Italian accent, "The next bleep, bleep, bleep, bleeping sandwich like that—fifteen dollars!"

The window sign came down first thing the next morning.

Kinds of media

When choosing a medium bear in mind that the public's taste is always changing. For example, newspaper readership is down compared to what it was in the sixties. It's still a good place to put some advertising dollars, but it sure isn't what it used to be. Do not buck trends!

Restaurants can use various media: daily newspapers, periodicals, community weeklies, school publications, radio, television, and coupon mailings, to name a few.

Large newspapers can be very effective. If a paper's readership is 200,000 people and one third of one percent respond to an ad, the business gains 600 customers. If the price of the ad is $1200, the ad costs $2.00 per customer.

The location of the ad is an important consideration. The entertainment section is read by people who have plans to go out and want to read about what's going on in town. The help-wanted section isn't

Small restaurants with a limited ad budget can use large newspapers with a plan that involves biannual promotions. Twice a year streak advertising can be effective. For example, $1200 could buy three straight days of loss-leader spots. The goal is to reach as many people as possible, with the hope of keeping some of the respondents as steady customers. This kind of high exposure has worked for many smaller restaurants.

Community publications. Town and community enterprises publish weekly or monthly newspapers, which offer a good and inexpensive means of exposure. These are excellent vehicles for value-related ads, because the readership lives near your restaurant. A full page can be bought very cheaply. In my experience, I have found very little difference between the professionalism and creative talent at small community papers and large city journals.

Spots in local high school, church, senior citizen, grange, hospital, and other community publications, too, are inexpensive, good advertising, and demonstrate support of worthwhile public activities.

Magazines. If the target audience is highly selective ("yuppies" for instance), the ad could go into one of the locally run magazines or trade publications.

Coupons. The American household is deluged with coupons, either through the mail or in almost every type of print media. Coupons usually offer a discount or a free item. They can be used to promote a new product or to gain new customers through the use of the loss leader technique. Larger restaurants, with a seating capacity of over 350 people, benefit most from a coupon promotion in large newspapers. Such a campaign usually generates an immediate and tremendous response. Make sure you can handle the traffic!

For the small facility, the alternative might be coupon packets that are mailed to homes in a particular area. The companies that design and mail the packets divide a city into a number of geographical mailing districts. They usually send 10,000 packets to each area. With this system, a manager can target an audience in a well-defined region. He or she can reach different locations on a set schedule (i.e., January, the northern section, June the west side, etc.).

Success can be gauged easily with coupon advertising. Just count the number of vouchers redeemed. If 10,000 are mailed for $360, and 1,000 are used, the effort has a ten percent success rate and each return costs the business 36¢.

Radio. While all print media advertising has a chance of being noticed at the convenience of the reader, a thirty-second radio spot can only be heard at the time it is being aired. A newspaper can be in the house all day long and can be picked up and read at any time. A potential reader of an ad could go out to the golf course for six hours, go shopping, come home, pick up the paper at his or her convenience, and notice a restaurant promotion. A potential customer could be listening to the radio for eight hours, but if he has to answer the phone at the wrong time, he will miss your commercial.

I had my first experience with radio advertising in the sixties. We ran a promotion in conjunction with a major golf tournament that came to our area. We spent $400 and got three responses. After that we tried radio on six separate occasions. None of the efforts worked. I am not an expert and I probably made many errors in technique; however, I always left the commercial's content in the hands of the experts at the local stations. I have my doubts about radio.

As recently as 1986, my restaurant spent $4000 in one month promoting loss leaders on the radio. We were on prime time, on what we were told was the "correct" easy-listening music station. In four weeks of polling our customers, eighty-six people said they heard the spots; of that number, forty-seven were steady customers who were not necessarily in the restaurant because of the ads. The net result was thirty-nine new patrons at a cost of $102.56 each.

I know of a retailer who says that he has great success with radio. He uses fifteen second spots repeated throughout the day. He sells tires. More power to him.

Television. Television, like radio, has a defined time within which an ad must be experienced. If you are not watching TV at a particular time, you won't see it. Of course there is the video recorder. But there is also fast forward.

Commercial time on television is very expensive; there is also the high cost of producing commercials. Perhaps with more cable network stations and more local programs competing for advertising dollars, TV exposure will become more affordable for the average restaurant. In my experience, however, television is not an effective medium for restaurant promotion.

Billboards. Billboards can be used by food establishments in an effective manner. The best place for this kind of display is in view of a heavily traveled road. Billboards are a 24-hour-a-day form of advertising and are not expensive, especially when contracted on a yearly basis. Theme and a coherent, limited message are important ingredients to the success of billboard ads:

> ## MICHAEL'S RESTAURANT—
> ## A GOOD REASON TO VISIT PLEASANTON

"Welcome, Neighbor" is a great concept for reaching new arrivals to the community. The Welcome Wagon is not the only company that lists names and addresses of newcomers for the purpose of promotion. Some deliver gifts or vouchers for free gifts from various subscribing merchants. The service fee and the gifts are supplied by the merchants. A restaurant can offer a gift certificate for specified amount of money (redeemable for food eaten at the facility), dinner for two, cocktails for two, discounts on certain meals, and so on.

Proper distribution of your ad budget

Once an ad budget is known, a definite plan using several media techniques must be devised. It is not a good idea to use only one type of advertising.

There is a restaurant known within the industry as the "Coupon Coop." Seventy-five percent of its business is through coupon ads. This is troubling. It is not good for any business to rely so heavily on one promotion. A restaurant should spotlight its food, service, and atmosphere in its marketing efforts. Its longevity depends on these factors, and not on gimmicks. Coupons can be a fad, and heavy reliance on them can prove to be a mistake in the long run.

Forecast your ad breakdown in percentages and stick to it as closely as possible. The following ad budget was used recently for a mid-sized restaurant in a suburban community:

- 20% large newspaper ads
- 25% local newspaper ads
- 15% promoting local good will through Little League programs, and high school weekly, etc.
- 20% community projects—charities, school needs, special police and town projects (giveaways at churches, grange, etc.)
- 20% coupon ads—Welcome Wagon, coupon mailings

Every restaurant must have an ad budget suitable to its location and its theme. It must be organized to bring about the best possible cost effectiveness. (Comprehensive advertising plans are nonexistent in most businesses, so taking the time to put one together will provide you with a competitive advantage.)

Helpful hints

Beware of advertising vendors who are less than truthful about who they represent. One business in our area was taking out an ad in a booklet that was supposedly published by the American Association for Youth Baseball (a legitimate charity). He always asked the solicitor if he represented the local Little League and the answer was always yes. He contributed $50 twice a year for five years until he found out that the drive was a swindle. He had been taken for a ride.

Always know the person to whom you hand money or a check. Make sure that the institution he or she claims to represent exists and is legitimate. Beware of advertising-related telephone solicitations from groups whose names seem imposing and authoritative, like the State Police, the Alcoholic Beverage Board, or other licensing entities. Ask for a phone number and check your directory.

Some salespeople use fear as a tool in the solicitation. They try to make the unsuspecting businessperson feel that his or her license might be in jeopardy if he or she doesn't purchase an ad. Licensing boards such as the Alcoholic Beverage Commission do not sell ads or collect money for charity. Advertising through local organizations *can* prove to be beneficial to a restaurant, but a manager must be aware that there is always the possibility of fraud. Investigate before buying an ad.

6

INVENTORY

6

INVENTORY

REASONS FOR INVENTORY

PEOPLE ITEMIZE OR CATEGORIZE THEIR GOODS AND POSSESSIONS for many different reasons. For example, one might compare what he or she has to what one's future needs might be. This is taking inventory, and it has been around since people have had possessions.

A good restaurant must have an effective inventory system in place to insure its success. Taking inventory is dull and boring, and too often it is a chore that is doled out to less-talented employees. Managers should insist on an effective inventory system and delegate the inventory work in a manner that emphasizes its importance.

Inventory is required for

1. the maintenance and freshness of food products,

2. the estimation of food and beverage costs,

3. the organization of kitchen labor,

4. the determination of loss through pilferage,

5. the protection of assets in the event of an insurance claim, whether through robbery, burglary, flood, or fire, and

6. to foster an effective purchasing system.

Before detailing inventory systems, let's look at what can happen when inventory is absent.

Pilferage

A life-long friend once confided to me that he felt he never made the kind of profit that reflected his volume of business or his pricing method. He felt sure that there was pilferage, but he could not quite identify when and how. Even though he sold food through a very limited menu, most of his business centered around his lounge and beverage sales. He asked me if I could try to help him identify the exact nature of the problem.

I arrived at his place on a Monday morning, at almost exactly the same time that he was getting a delivery from a liquor and beer vendor. My friend and I talked while he was receiving and counting the goods against the invoice. When the truck left we went into his office. I asked what was going to happen to the newly arrived stock. He told me that "some kid" was coming in later in the day and was going to put it into the storage room. I suddenly realized what was wrong, and it wasn't necessarily that this kid was stealing booze. My friend simply did not have an inventory system; therefore anyone who had access to the storage room (which meant just about every employee) could have been robbing him blind.

He put an inventory system in place and his beverage costs went from 34 percent to 21 percent in one month.

My friend was a good businessman. He was good at buying, selling, public relations, and keeping his books in order. However, he lacked just one important system that kept him from achieving the profits he deserved.

There is an interesting follow-up to this. Obviously, the theft that had been occurring was done primarily by employees. A year later, his staff was made up of most of the same employees! The inventory system made it virtually impossible to take something without arousing suspicion. The problem just vanished without conflict or any dip in morale.

Insurance

I remember being told of a string of burglaries in a downtown area. One restaurant was hit for quite a bit of goods. The burglars were caught and pleaded guilty, but in recounting what they had loaded onto their van, they denied taking four cases of Scotch from the restaurant. The police told the burglars that even if they admitted to the four cases of Scotch, it wouldn't add any more punishment. But they *didn't* admit to it. Because of the police report, the insurance company refused to compensate the restaurant for the four cases of Scotch. The main reason was that there was no record of inventory, even though there was evidence of purchase through invoice records. Obviously, adequate insurance is vital; keeping good inventory goes hand in hand with your other protective measures.

INVENTORY TECHNIQUES

There has been a reclassification of restaurants as manufacturing enterprises by the federal government. There is very good reason for this position. Restaurants, like factories, take bulk or raw products, combine them with other raw products, process them and change their form, and then sell them. With this in mind, an inventory system for a restaurant would work much the same as for any manufacturing plant.

If one thinks of a restaurant as a manufacturing plant, there are two basic categories of goods and two basic types of inventory.

1. Inventory of the bulk raw product that is received and stored and is still in the original bulk form, such as a case of U25 headless shrimp. (This is bulk inventory.)

2. Inventory of items that have been taken out of bulk form, have been processed, and are being readied for consumption, such as U25 headless shrimp that have been shelled and deveined. (This is the chef's inventory.)

Bulk inventory

For the purpose of bulk inventory, the restaurant must have a list of all products used in food prep and beverage areas.

Standardized inventory sheets should be typed and clear. The expense of purchasing or having printed sheets that are particular to a restaurant will be quickly offset by the benefits of clear, concise inventory. Bulk listing should be a weekly event, preferably on Monday morning before salespeople arrive and purchase orders are placed. (See Figs. 11-A & 11-B)

Inventory sheets should be set up according to the various storage areas, for example, all grocery items should be on the same page or general area of the sheet. All items should be classified in the same way that the vendor identifies them on the invoices, for example, white meat tuna by the case (cs). The sheet

GROCERY INVENTORY WORKSHEET FOR THE WEEKS OF: _____ PAGE ___

DRY GOODS	IN STOCK	REC'D	TOTAL		IN STOCK	REC'D	TOTAL
ELBOW MACARONI							
FETTUCINI							
LASAGNA							
LINGUINI							
ORZO							
RAINBOW ROTINI							
SPAGHETTINI							
SPINACH FETTUCINI							
THIN SPAGHETTI							
ZITI							
DE-CAF COFFEE							
MAYONNAISE							
MUSHROOMS (CANNED)							
PEPPERONCINI							
TUNA							
HOT CHOPPED PEPPERS							
RED WINE VINEGAR							
RELISH							
RUSSIAN DRESSING							

FIGURE 11-A

GROCERY INVENTORY WORKSHEET (cont.)   PAGE

DRY GOODS	IN STOCK	REC'D	TOTAL	IN STOCK	REC'D	TOTAL
CHOCOLATE SAUCE						
CLARET SAUCE						
DUCK SAUCE						
MOLASSES						
SOY SAUCE						
BATTER MIX						
CORNMEAL						
CROUTONS						
KETCHUP (BTLS)						
KETCHUP (PACKETS)						
NUTRA-MATE						
PREMIUM SALTINES						
RITZ (CRUSHED)						

FIGURE 11-B

should have room for four or five weeks of inventory. This helps determine if there is any overstocking. A typical inventory sheet looks something like this:

Inventory Sheet					
	Nov. 1	Nov. 8	Nov. 15	Nov. 22	Nov. 29
White Meat Tuna	3½ cs.	4 cs.	3 cs.	——————	——————
Ketchup	1 cs.	1¼ cs.	¼ cs.	——————	——————
Canned Peas	2 cs.	3 cs.	1½ cs.	——————	——————

FIGURE 12

Product location

To encourage precise inventory, the stock should be well organized in the various storage areas (walk-in refrigerators, freezers, grocery storage rooms, vegetable storage rooms, locked up liquor and beer rooms, and nonfood storage areas for napkins, glassware, silverware, paper goods, and aprons). All stockrooms should have names that are readily identifiable to all employees. Too often, a relatively new employee in a restaurant is sent to bring back a particular item and comes back empty handed because he or she misunderstood where to look for the item. Small signs identifying each storage area are beneficial to both employees and delivery people, and will help you manage inventory more effectively.

To expedite the inventory process, place goods in the storage areas as they appear on the inventory sheet. Placing products in a designated place is a must in keeping accurate inventory.

Product rotation

When stock is properly rotated, a restaurant's bulk inventory is usually neatly placed and categorized. Counting items becomes more efficient and more accurate. The result is an inventory that is accurate, and a more efficient buying process.

Product rotation is important in assuring product freshness. Make sure that all employees get used to putting new goods behind and underneath older goods. One can also color code goods as they are being delivered. For example, all goods received on the first week of the month could be marked with a red marking pen, the second week in blue, and so forth.

An accurate bulk inventory is a necessary first step to insuring an efficient buying system.

Chef's inventory

Examples of food products that are not in bulk form include sugar that has been placed in sugar bowls; meat that has been taken out of packaging and trimmed, portioned, and readied for cooking; all opened bottles, whether they contain foods or beverages; and all prepared foods that have been processed on the premises. These products generally are ready for consumption and sale, and should be under very strict inventory control by the chef or bartender. Most of these items are physically close to the line cooks in the kitchen.

The chef should have an inventory sheet (See Fig. 13) for these goods, one that has each item listed under a day of the week. In this way, the inventory can be estimated daily. It is difficult to be precise with most processed foods. For example, it would not be practical to measure the exact number of quarts left in a ten-quart container of chicken soup. Generally, an estimate (such as, one-half of a container) is a sufficient approximation for the purposes of this inventory.

The chef's inventory is important in determining:

1. the production schedule,
2. use of highly stocked goods as specials, and
3. assuring freshness and preventing spoilage.

This inventory should be compared to the bulk inventory once a week to ensure all of the goals mentioned above are being met.

Organizational procedures that foster an efficient inventory are:

1. storing foods in defined locations
2. consolidating food whenever possible, and
3. rotating the product.

Each type of food should occupy a designated place in kitchen storage areas. Many food storage containers look alike; it is an inefficient use of labor to have workers spending time looking through many containers to find particular products. All food containers should be readily identifiable. This can be accomplished by having products placed in designated areas with identifying

CHEF'S INVENTORY

IN STOCK	SUN.	MON.	TUES.	WED.	THURS.	FRI.	SAT.
6 OZ. HAMBURGERS WRAPPED							
ONION SOUP (GALLON)							
COOKED VEGETABLES (BUCKET)							
COOKED RICE (CONTAINER)							
CUT STEAKS (# PORTION)							
FILLET HADDOCK (# PORTION)							
VEAL (# PORTION)							
CHICKEN (# PORTION)							
EGGPLANT (TRAY)							
COOKED PASTA (BUCKET)							
LASAGNA (# PORTION)							
GRAVIES (BUCKET)							
MOZZARELLA CHEESE (# PACKAGE)							
COLESLAW (BUCKET)							

FIGURE 13

labels. This not only helps in inventory control, it eliminates needless work and waste.

Whenever possible, products should be consolidated. It is not unusual to walk into a kitchen and find three different containers, each one-third full of the same product. This practice leads to poor use of storage space and inefficient inventory analysis.

The wait staff should be responsible for consolidating items that are specific to their areas. There are many items that only service personnel work with (such as napkins, sugar packets, and set-up materials).

And, as we have noted, all personnel should get into the habit of rotating stock, so that the older items are used first. To help in this endeavor, the chef should have all prepared foods labeled, with a date and time of preparation. This not only aids inventory, it assures that customers are less likely to be served rancid or soured foods.

An organized inventory of the prepared and processed foods in the kitchen is a great help when reordering items. Later in this chapter we will discuss the chef's maintenance of inventory control levels.

Liquor inventory

When establishments hire detectives, most of their effort is concentrated on liquor control. Why? Two good reasons: liquor is expensive and it's dangerous. Liquor control is a perennial problem in every restaurant I know. Some places have resorted to very expensive computerized pouring systems. This helps control liquor at the bar, but doesn't solve all the problems. Many restaurants have surveillance cameras focused on both the serving area and storage room. There are places with elaborate jail bars and lockup systems, where storage areas resemble prison cells.

An employee who is old enough to work but too young to drink can cause the restaurant to lose its license if he or she gains, consumes or steals liquor. In most cases, employees do not steal booze for financial gain. They drink it themselves, share it with other people, or take it home for a party.

My conclusion is that all liquor bottles must be marked and identified individually. This is not going to be foolproof, but just imagine the chaos if a principal did not have a list of students and assigned classrooms. Though a school has many rooms, there are only three possible places for a bottle: in the storage room, at the bar, or empty in a place where it can be identified and checked off the list. (See Fig. 14)

TALLY OF LIQUOR USED

FOR THE WEEK OF: _____

NOTE: Each day is divided into 2 sections ONE SECTION FOR DAY SHIFT and ONE SECTION FOR
        NIGHT SHIFT.

RECORD BOTTLES YOU BRING UP FROM LIQUOR ROOM ONLY

MISC	MON		TUES		WED		THU		FRI		SAT		SUN		TOTAL

FIGURE 14

Let's examine an efficient method of identifying each bottle with a simple code. Assume that it is the first week of the month, and among the liquor being received are two cases (or twenty-four bottles) of Jack Daniels. The code for Jack Daniels could be A or JD or any other simple symbol that identifies brand. A number code for this particular delivery would run from between one and twenty-four because that is the number of bottles that were received. Next, you need to identify the week the bottles arrived. Since there can be no more than five weeks in a month the week symbol can be a number from one to five. This particular order was received during the first week of the month, so the symbol would be one.

Mark each bottle with its code. The mechanics are simple. When putting the bottles on the shelf, mark each one according to the order of placement. For example, the twelfth bottle would be marked, "jd-12-1". On an inventory sheet with columns that run vertically and horizontally, one can easily list all the bottles in stock.

As liquor is moved from the stockroom to serving areas, a marking should be made in the appropriate place on the stock list to indicate that a particular bottle has been removed from storage and is now at the bar. This marking could be a slash, circle, or any other easy-to-mark symbol. Of course, there needs to be a stock sheet copy in the storage area. The person in charge of inventory must transfer the information from the list at the storage area to his or her own list on a daily basis. If this is done faithfully, the manager will know where every bottle is.

The concept is simple. If you identify each item, it's got to be somewhere in the restaurant. If it isn't in storage, if it isn't at the bar, and if it hasn't been crossed off as empty, what happened or who took it? With a system like this, a manager is reacting in a knowledgeable manner about losses and not just guessing. If you wait until the bank balance dips, the reaction is "If I catch anyone stealing, I'll kill him." This kind of outburst does not stop pilferage.

It takes about fifteen minutes a day to keep a systematic inventory as described above, but it can save thousands of dollars.

Par inventory

Most well-managed properties have a predetermined number of bottles of each type of liquor at the bar at all times. This inventory control system resembles the chef's zero inventory mentioned above. This process is called a Par Inventory. Empty bottles are checked out of the inventory journal and discarded by the bar manager at the end of each shift and replaced by full bottles from the stockroom. With this system, a manager is able to monitor the amount of liquor used during a shift and compare that with the gross liquor sales.

All bottles that are empty and checked out of stock on an inventory sheet should also be destroyed or marked with a large black X across the front of the bottle. In some establishments where this is not done, empty bottles have a strange way of reappearing at the bar as part of the par inventory.

OTHER INVENTORY ISSUES

Locating a problem

A consultant told me of a restaurant that was doing a nice business, had a good reputation, was owner-managed, and seemed to be well run. The reason the consultant was hired was that the expected profits were not being realized. He hired a couple of detectives to look into the possibility of inside theft. There were some giveaways at the bar, but nothing excessive and nothing the owner had not already accounted for. Certainly there was not enough to have a real effect on the cost product to sales formula. The inventory system was nearly perfect. There was good security in the storage area. Utility costs were in line. Menu pricing was thorough and well done, with the prospect for good profit. Labor costs were in the 27% range and were consistent for a whole year. Purchasing was not a problem; the owner did the buying and had a knack for getting good prices. The chef was good and there was hardly any waste in the production process. A solid restaurant that was just not making the projected profit—there didn't seem to be an explanation.

Two weeks after he submitted his analysis, the consultant happened to run into a supplier who had this particular restaurant as a client. During their conversation the supplier said, "Boy, do they go through register tapes," referring to their mutual client. Suddenly, there was something to investigate. The consultant went back to the restaurant owner and asked him to count the register tapes. It turned out that he was definitely using one third more than normal.

A two-week investigation solved the problem. The night manager, who was responsible for the night deposit, was clearing the register, removing the portion of the tape that dealt with the day's business, and then entering a whole new group of sales on the register. It was now very easy for him to pocket the difference between the actual sales and the lower sales total that he invented. In the morning when the owner removed the part of the tape that he thought represented the previous day's sales, he had no reason to be suspicious: the total on the tape invariably matched the total on the bank deposit. The angry owner's reaction to all of this: "The bastard was even too cheap to buy his own tape; if he had, he never would have been caught."

Stock control

Quality control engineers and inventory experts in large manufacturing plants talk of maintaining zero inventory. In this sense, zero does not mean that they are completely out of stock. Rather it means that the zero line is the ideal line that insures a minimum amount of stock on hand, while ensuring that there is no danger of running out of stock of any item.

In most businesses, it's up to the inventory engineer to determine what level of stock constitutes "zero" for each item. He or she usually relies on past data (such as previous years' sales, production efficiency, and monthly or weekly inventory levels).

The restaurant manager can duplicate this type of inventory analysis. It is important for a restaurant to achieve zero-inventory levels for the same reasons it is important to a large manufacturing plant; what's more, spoilage is a problem. Therefore, the trick is to determine what the acceptable maximum and minimum levels of stock should be and to strike the average between the two, calling that number zero. Consideration must be given to determine the delivery day, when the required stock has to last for up to a week. The zero level occurs ideally on the date of delivery.

Let's assume that a restaurant sells eighteen sirloin strips a week on average, but has sold as many as twenty-one on several occasions. You don't want to run out at any time, so at the end of the week when twenty-one are sold, you still want to have one left over. That dictates that twenty-two steaks would be ideal at the beginning of the week to avoid running out. Since eighteen is the average, the middle point between twenty-two and eighteen is twenty. Twenty is the mean. Since $22 - 20 = 2$ and $20 - 18 = 2$, zero inventory in terms of sirloins is two. Therefore the aim is to have two sirloins left at delivery time. Unfortunately, most of the time there will be four left over, because the average sold is eighteen. This is far from a perfect science, but just remember that this type of inventory control is dictated by two opposing forces. One, it is ideal never to run out of any food items; and two, it is great to have limited stock.

In terms of the chef's inventory the zero level should occur at the end of the day. Ideally you don't have a lot left over, but you also do not want to refuse a customer a menu item.

Why must a chef's inventory be taken daily?

1. The volume of business varies depending on the day of the week. Weekends are generally busier than weekdays.

2. Menu items sell better on some days than on other days. This is usually determined by past performance. In general more fish and less beef is sold on Fridays.

3. Specials have an effect on menu items. If Veal Marsala were a board special, this should result in diminished sales of other veal dishes.

Inventory and production schedules are intertwined. Achieving good product controls depends on having a good production schedule, and vice versa.

Use of computers

Computers work well in established chains where menus are limited, almost everything is portioned when delivered, and each sale represents a reduction of stock that can be easily calculated. For example, all of McDonald's quarter-pound hamburgers are counted in numbers (one case has 100 quarter pounders). If sales indicate that 850 were sold and 1000 were in stock, there should be 150 left.

On the other hand, if a restaurant with a full menu had Salisbury Steak, hamburgers, and meatloaf on the menu and with one inventory stating that 100 pounds of hamburger were ordered, the unit sales on hamburger products would only help one estimate how many pounds of hamburger would be left.

In general, the more creative and complex the cooking procedure, the less valuable a computer is in determining inventory based on sales. A precise system in a creative kitchen requires terminals in all food preparation areas and kitchen help trained to make precise entries into the computer about exactly what was used in preparation or processing. This is often impractical.

Many of the computers used in restaurants *are* invaluable tools in evaluating food costs, popularity of food items, and ideal purchasing percentages (e.g., if 10 percent of sales were white fish, then ideally 10 percent of purchases should be white fish). All of this information must be used in conjunction with a good bulk-inventory system and a chef's inventory. (The more creative and diverse a restaurant is, the more the need for good inventory control.) The best computer still requires humans to count stock and make the computer entries.

Once goods have been counted and recorded the computer can be valuable in storing inventory information and for making comparisons of week-to-week levels of product left over.

An aid in determining gross profit

In large restaurants—especially those that are part of a hotel complex—weekly inventory is used to assess the gross profit. This helps to determine whether the sales ideals have been achieved. An analysis is done—usually by the controller—in which the invoices of goods received are matched with the inventory against gross food sales and gross beverage sales. A meeting is then held with the general manager, the controller, the chef, the buyer, and the food and beverage managers, in which they discuss the data. If the ideal ratio of food costs to food sales is 27 percent, and the data shows food costs at 34 percent, there is likely to be hell to pay at the meeting. The general manager seeks answers from each department to find the source of the problem. The underlying causes could range from excessive spoilage to a tremendous and sudden boost in food costs.

Inventory helps to determine food costs in the following manner. Suppose three sirloins were part of the previous week's inventory and eighteen were received during the week. This adds up to twenty-one sirloins in stock. This week's inventory shows two sirloins left. That means that nineteen have been sold. Assuming that sirloins average thirteen pounds each and the cost per pound on the current invoice is $3.19, the total cost of the sirloins sold is $787.93. This cost is added to all other food costs and the results are the total food costs, which can then be compared to the total food sales.

Can the small restaurant be this sophisticated in the use of inventory data? The answer is yes. It *has* to be this sophisticated to survive.

The smaller establishment can use the mechanics described above even if manpower considerations dictate that it can only be done once a month. Inventory analysis helps to determine what a restaurant's problems might be and how to isolate them. No one can solve a problem unless it is identified. Saying, "I'm losing money," is like saying, "I have a sickness." But saying, "I'm losing money on beef products," is like saying, "I have a headache." When one isolates the symptoms one can obtain a prescription that can alleviate the pain.

One can see the importance of the chef's inventory remaining as close to the zero level as possible. If there is a glut of stock in the processed inventory, it throws off the results of the analysis of gross profit or the percentages of food costs.

Enhancing purchasing

When inventory levels of certain products rise or fall, either because of increased or decreased sales of a particular menu item, the chef and the buyer can use this information to project future initiatives. The chef might work toward more innovation in creating specials around beef products or any other menu laggards.

The buyer uses inventory to decide the amount of product that must be purchased. If he or she notices that certain prices are going to dip, the inventory levels of certain products might be raised.

When all aspects of inventory systems are in place and working correctly, spoilage decreases, the buyer can make the best use of company funds, kitchen efficiency increases, costs are kept in line, and profits increase.

7

PURCHASING

7

PURCHASING

THE WORLD OF RESTAURANT PURCHASING

I WAS HIRED BY A REAL-ESTATE DEVELOPER TO ANALYZE DATA AND make projections for a new restaurant he was building. He owned several other restaurants that were losing money, and my first impression was that he would only dig a deeper hole by expanding. He contradicted my fear by saying that he really wanted to turn everything around and make all of his food enterprises profitable. He also asked if I would take a look at some of his other restaurants during my analysis.

I agreed, and the very first day on the job we met over breakfast. He told me about his general manager. We'll call her Florence Freeman. With great inflection and excitement in his voice, he told me that Mrs. Freeman was the greatest administrator that he had ever known, had ever heard of! And then, his eyes lighting up, he said, "Well, maybe Golda Meir is better." And then he sort of came back to earth and looked at me and recanted: "No, Florence is better!"

Well, you can bet that I was very anxious to meet Mrs. Freeman, but at the same time there was an inescapable question. Why were they losing money? The place seemed to be falling apart!

I met with her that afternoon and we exchanged all of the niceties. Then she pointed at me and said, "The one thing that you can't interfere with is our buying system. We have the best. We buy all of our meats from one vendor who always gives us the best deals because we buy in such quantity."

Well, I certainly was not going to touch the purchasing system. With that kind of assurance coming from a potential world leader, there would be no need for my advice. I knew where she was coming from and I was going to leave well enough alone.

About a week later, I got some invoices from the controller as an aid in pricing out a new menu. I couldn't believe it! Some of the meat prices seemed so outrageous that I just had to investigate. True to my suspicions, when the comparison was made between the prices they were paying, and the prices on commodity sheets of other vendors, they were getting ripped off to the tune of over $2,500 a week. Not exactly small change!

Their invoices also had many instances of round weights. It is unlikely that pieces of meat could be cut exactly to weigh ten pounds. If one were to order two pounds of steak from a butcher, he or she would put a piece on the scale, and the weight would be around, but very seldom exactly, two pounds. Their invoices read 75 pounds ribs, 150 pounds sirloins, 80 pounds top butt. These invoices were loaded with questionable entries. Sirloins vary in weight and a more believable reading would have been 147.903 pounds. This is the kind of weight usually found on an invoice. There was also a lack of specifications on most products.

CLEAR INVOICE READING

NO.	TYPE	BRAND	WEIGHT	PORTION
15	1x1 choice sirloin	I.B.P.	147.387 lbs.	$2.85 lb.

Total Price $420.05

FIGURE 15

Their invoice read:

15	Sirloin	150 lbs	$3.00 lb.

Total $450.00

FIGURE 16

Note the lack of product yield, type, brand, and so on.

This makes for an impossible receiving system. Specifications and qualifications become a guessing game.

What kind of an effect did my discovery make on this group of restaurants?

Well, you can't fight city hall! However, a little while after I finished my work, someone told me that my recommendations were put to good use.

One of the reasons this establishment did not have a dynamic purchasing system was because the chef, who was the buyer of all food products, was not given enough discretion. He was told to deal with specific companies for specific products and no one else. The vendor, theoretically, was supplying products according to the restaurant's own specs.

When a restaurant is married to its food specs, there is more of a chance of collusion between buyer and vendor. Since there is no competition, and the restaurant is buying certain products from only one supplier, there is a good chance of price inflation and kickbacks to cooperating buyers.

Buying exclusively according to restaurant specs assumes that the receiver has the specification book open, and is skilled enough to look at a case of tenderloins and identify the meats according to the prescribed standards. This is more dream than reality.

I know a lot of good cooks who have a tough time distinguishing between the various cuts of meat. Restaurant specifications should be a *general* guide to the kind of products used in a particular restaurant, and not etched in stone so that a buyer is prevented from using his or skills to purchase good quality products at good prices. If a buyer has a good system, he can eliminate all the guesswork from the receiving process.

Most meat products are packed in the Midwest, where they are graded, packed, boxed, and labeled according to very specific identification standards. For example, a case of ribs may be labeled "I.B.P.—Choice Boneless Eye Two-Inch Lip," with an accompanying vendor code number, such as #11754. If a purchaser gives this kind of information to the receiver, he is relying on a simple method of product identification. If the label is right, the product should be right. (Most people who check in orders do not have the expertise to distinguish between a rib eye and a sirloin.)

It is illegal for most vendors to break seals on the boxes before shipping. The product that is identified on the label must be the product that is in the case. The only purveyors who can open boxes are those with federal inspectors within their plants. These packers have the right to break cases and packaging, trim meats, and repack them under their own labels.

When beef is shipped to a restaurant with labeling that reads, "six rib eyes," and no other specifications, it takes an expert to determine the exact quality of the meat. In some of the restaurants I have worked with, I have seen meat of inferior quality being bought at top prices. In all these restaurants, the vendor was supposed to be supplying meat according to the restaurant specs. The buyer and receiver were not qualified to determine what the actual grade or price range should have been for a particular product.

The exact identity of product should be clear both on the packaging and invoice. This is the only way one can compare the prices of similar products and ensure the best buying posture for a restaurant.

Trust

Many buyers—and even chefs—feel inferior in determining quality. They feel threatened when dealing with salespeople. They look for what they consider to be one honest vendor, whom they can trust and to whom they can give their business. Invariably, they pay more for their product than they would if they allowed for more competition when purchasing. It is not against the law for salespeople to charge higher prices when they can. Greed is part of the system and will always exist. My father used to say, "It's up to you to keep him honest!"

A good buyer is a lot like a good salesperson and must be the equal of a salesperson during the purchasing encounter. Good buyers enjoy a persistent seller, because his ego will not let the sale get away no matter what the cost. If a buyer can be strong of character, he or she will get more information about the product and better buys from an assertive salesperson than from a weaker one. If the buyer has a weak personality, he or she will usually be "eaten alive" by the stronger salesperson, but will not fare that much better with a weaker one.

There was a salesman who represented a very large company I had dealt with for years; had a reputation for being a little shifty. He was known to change prices after giving a quote to inflate orders on occasion. Everyone, whether a restaurateur or salesperson, knew this guy as "Tank Turkey." He had quite a reputation and quite an ego. He was the best salesman in his branch, and there was good reason for this. He was as persistent in getting sales as anyone I've ever seen, and as knowledgeable about product as any executive chef.

When we were dealing with Tank Turkey, we had to record every price he quoted, and have a precise record of the order. That way we avoided surprises. We were always prepared with price lists from several other companies and got as much information as we could about future prices. We were well equipped to deal with him and the result was usually very good prices compared to the prices paid by other restaurants in our area. He would sell to us at such a low price that he would lose his commission in many cases. His ego would not allow him to lose a sale to another company. He did well with us, but we did well with him, also.

A well-organized buyer can help a restaurant make money. He or she must have certain skills, and must be able to interact with the chef and the food-and-beverage supervisors. A good buyer must have

1. product knowledge,

2. the pure and simple savvy about the art of buying,

3. an honest character and an interest in the establishment (to make collusion with vendors less likely), and

4. an assertive personality to get the best possible prices.

A buyer's function is to assure quality products at low cost, a twin goal that is essential for a profitable restaurant.

OBSTACLES TO PURCHASING

Buying is not a perfect science; there are selling techniques that can become obstacles to effective buying. The purchaser must be aware of the methods that might be detrimental to the buying process. The negatives associated with buying include:

1. salespeople pawning inferior products

2. low balling

3. salespeople stimulating overstocking or glutting

4. salespeople quoting inaccurate product and price.

Most salespeople are decent, honest people, but a buyer should not be concerned with a seller's morality or personality. Rather he or she should be constantly aware and be able to identify the negative techniques listed above to ensure that they are not part of the buying encounter.

Inferior products

An inferior product is one whose yield or quality is less than that of a competitive product. A salesperson who tries to pawn off inferior products in a restaurant is probably trying to impress upon the buyer that he has the lowest prices (a case of sirloins can have a price spread of $2.00 from the highest grade [Primes] to the lowest restaurant grade [Standard]). Every salesperson is working to beat the competition, and the easiest way to do this is to quote low prices without precise qualifications. Often, the salesperson will tend to generalize about products rather than use specifics. For example, a salesperson might try to sell a case of light meat tuna without explaining how many cans of tuna there are in a case, what the yield of each can is, whether the tuna is packed in oil or water, or who the packer is. In general, you can expect a salesperson to talk only of the positive qualities of a product and leave out the negative qualities.

Another method salespeople use to influence buyers to purchase low cost, but lower grade, products is the "key word" approach. A salesperson might say that "good grade" ribs are on sale. The word *good* in this case might refer to the grading system in which the meat's acceptability is next to the bottom as a restaurant rib. The word *imported* is also used quite often to influence a buyer. For some reason, imported ham sounds better than domestic ham when, in fact, many imported ham products are far inferior to domestic products.

A salesperson might purposely leave out any mention of yield. Yield is the amount that is actually used for public consumption after trimming. Yield and weight of a product are not necessarily the same thing. Keeping this in mind, one must always be wary of extremely low prices for any products. For an example, meats can vary from 60 percent to 96 percent yield. A case of lettuce, to use another example, might yield anywhere from 90 percent for solid heads to less than 50 percent for smaller, looser heads. There are usually 24 heads of lettuce in a case, and the case is the generally accepted unit.

Canned products can vary in yield depending on product weight and water weight in each can. A salesperson knows everything regarding the comparisons between yield, weight, and unit selling (such as by the dozen, case, pounds, etc.); therefore, it is necessary for a buyer to be equally informed.

Low balling

Buyers must understand that every salesperson who comes in to solicit an account is working to make a commission and money for his/her company. The buyer must accept this and yet still get the best overall bargain for the restaurant. There isn't a vendor who gives products away, and there isn't a salesperson who will service a restaurant week after week without making a commission.

Generally, the commission a salesperson is working for is in the neighborhood of 2.5 percent. There are higher and lower commission items, but the average order amounts to 2.5 percent commission. For example, if the total cost of goods is $1,000, the commission for the salesperson is about $25.00. A salesperson can increase the commission by charging high prices for big-dollar items. The seller's price list has a high and a low that can be charged for each item. If the seller can convince the buyer that he/she is giving an item away at cost, and that item is a low-cost item (such as 30 percent off on a $10.00 box of crackers) and then get the highest price on two cases of prime rib (total weight 170 pounds at 10¢ per pound higher than the medium price on his list), there is a net loss for the buyer (in this case, $14.00).

```
$17 overpayment on ribs
— $3 savings on crackers
== $14 overcharge
```

FIGURE 17

The sales encounter described above is a form of low balling. The salesperson tries to impress the buyer with the notion that his/her prices are far lower than any competitors', in order to grab the biggest piece of the pie for himself.

A salesperson introducing himself to a new account might use low balling in a more outrageous manner. Here's how it might work: For the first few weeks, the rep cuts prices so drastically that he makes no commissions. He tries to dupe the buyer into believing that no other company can compete with his. He hopes to get the total order week after week, thus driving the competition away. If he succeeds, he gradually increases his prices and makes up his initial losses. With the competition gone, this person can make a killing, all at the expense of the restaurant. At this point, the buyer *thinks* he is getting the best possible prices around, while he is actually stuffing the pockets of the seller. (Remember that a 3 percent overcharge per week totals up to thousands of dollars over a period of a year.)

Glutting

A seller is always interested in increasing the total order. The larger the order, the greater the commission, and the less business for the competition. If the seller can influence the buyer to overstock an item, the seller will not have to compete in selling that product for a while.

Salespeople use different methods when convincing a buyer to glut the stockroom. If the seller knows a restaurant has enough of an item, the "Journal approach" might come into play. "You'd better buy more of it now; I read somewhere, I think it was *The Wall Street Journal*, that the price is going to skyrocket." Or he/she might use the "volume buy:" "If you buy enough, you'll save tons of money."

If the seller succeeds in either one of these sales methods, the result is

1. a storage area that is glutted with product, causing inefficient space management,

2. the possibility of increased energy costs, if refrigeration is required, and

3. a less efficient inventory analysis.

Usually there will not be substantial enough savings to warrant overstocking. A strong effort to attain zero inventory levels will prevent overstocking. Resistance to high-pressure sales techniques is essential. If there seems to be a reason to inflate stock levels, the purchaser should involve the chef and top management in the decision.

Inappropriate product

In recent years, due to advances in food processing techniques, the food industry has been saturated with new products. It is the duty of every salesperson to introduce these items to clients. New products generally offer higher commissions to the vendors. As a result, some salespeople become so overzealous that they show no interest in whether a product is suited to a particular restaurant. A buyer, on the other hand, must not succumb to pressure tactics from vendors on this score, but must be sure about the appropriateness of a product. A careless buyer ends up with products on the shelf that are never used. This eventually leads to all of the problems associated with overstocking.

Intentional price misquotation

An unethical ploy used by some salespeople is planned price changing. This is a method in which quoted prices are changed to higher commission prices when the order is placed with the wholesale company. In this type of deceit, the salesperson hopes that the buyer will forget the quoted price by the time the delivery is made, or that the invoice will not be checked for prices. A buyer who does not have pencil in hand marking the quoted prices is an easy target of this scam. Again, this activity is not performed by all salespeople, but it is done often enough to warrant caution.

A GOOD PURCHASING SYSTEM

Implementing a good purchasing system is not easy. It requires skill and knowledge on the buyer's part as well as a judicious attitude toward salespeople. When a salesperson is caught low balling, for instance, you may be tempted to discontinue the relationship entirely. If this is done, it is not only the salesperson who is thrown out, but also the company, the price lists, and the products the company supplies, all of which might benefit your restaurant. And that's not to mention any beneficial information the seller might have access to. Instead, the salesperson should be closely watched. It's not the salesperson who costs the restaurant money, it's the unskilled buyer.

Once one knows some of the negative-selling techniques, the next step is to establish an organized buying system. To develop a good purchasing method, a buyer must have

1. a ready, thorough knowledge of inventory,

2. a definite time schedule to meet with various salespeople,

3. knowledge of product,

4. general knowledge of current prices, and

5. a limited and systemized method of telephone ordering.

Knowledge of inventory

Assuming that a proper inventory system has been established and that a proper inventory has been taken, a list of items to be ordered should be made prior to the arrival of your salesperson. This list should consider anticipated specials to run that week. When a buyer is prepared to buy, he saves time during the sales session. Since he knows what he wants, he concentrates on getting the best possible quality and prices. These determinations should be made in consultation with the chef.

Time schedule

Time schedules should be set up with all salespeople. This insures a steady delivery schedule and a planned number of hours to be devoted to purchasing. This is because purchasing schedules lead to efficient use of time—especially in small restaurants, where the buyer is also the chef, personnel manager, and all around fill-in person. A definite time schedule with all salespeople is often very hard to achieve, but as it is with most things of this nature, the squeaky wheel tends to get the grease.

Product knowledge

Product knowledge is a must. I have been shocked to find out how many restaurant managers—and even chefs—don't know the difference between a 109 rib and a rib eye. When purchasing meats, a buyer should know the type of meat, its purchase name, its menu name, its grade, its yield code, and how all of these affect the price. Following are some grades of sirloin.

Meat Type	Menu Name	Grade	Yield Code	Price
Sirloin	Sirloin steak	Prime	1x1	highest
Sirloin	Broiled steak	Prime	1x1	highest
Sirloin	Broiled steak	Choice	1x1	high
Sirloin	Broiled steak	Choice	2x3	medium high
Sirloin	Broiled or roast (less tender)	Good	1x1	medium
Sirloin	Broiled or roast (less tender)	Ungraded (no blue streak)	1x1	medium low
Sirloin	Broiled or roast (less tender)	ungraded	2x3	low

FIGURE 18

Fat marbling in red meat helps determine grade. Along with the amount of fat, yield grade is supposedly a determination of fat content.

Meat packers determine whether the meats are to be graded. Some meat packers sell no-rolls. The meat is inspected for interstate delivery, but is not graded by the inspector. Those that are graded have a distinctive blue streak on the back side or the fat side of the meat. 1x1 or 2x2 refers to the tip size, which is mainly composed of solid fat. All types of meats have similar grade and yield codes. A buyer should post charts that rate the types of meat used in the restaurant.

Relevant information, facts, and charts should be procured and kept in a convenient place so that they can be referred to during the buying session. Meats, groceries, produce, frozen goods, seafood products, liquor, beer and wine, and all nonfood products should be categorized according to their relative price structure. For example, white meat canned tuna is generally more expensive than light meat canned tuna. When purchasing canned tomato products, you should bear in mind that Mediterranean canned tomatoes are usually better than those canned in California, Italy, Israel, or Spain. But remember that even high-quality products must also be judged according to yield.

It is impossible to list all the relative price structures for all restaurant products in this book. Below is a list of sources for information about grades and yields of various products.

USDA Meat Buyer's Guide

Professional Cooking, by Wayne Gisslen, John Wiley and Sons.

Commodity Lists, printed by Hallsmith-Sysco, Inc.

publications by Sexton, Inc.

publications by Kraft, Inc.

FIGURE 19

Ask salespeople about these publications.

The best way to buy newly marketed products is in very small quantities. Before placing an order, ask

1. if there is a free sample of the product available,

2. the names of restaurants already using the product,

3. for the exact ingredients or processing methods, and

4. if it is appropriate for your restaurant.

Knowledge of current and quoted prices

At the beginning of each week a buyer should call several vendors and get a general idea of what to expect for prices for the week. From week to week, certain meat, produce, and seafood products will fluctuate in price. Too many buyers jump at the first good-looking deal they can get, without having a sense of the overall market. For example, if haddock prices are down because of a good catch, the buyer who knows this will be better prepared to get the best deal.

Some suppliers make available a weekly price list. Insist that you get your copy before the seller arrives. In this way, you can write listed prices on your order sheet and get a head start in dealing with your seller. The salesperson will be less apt to low ball or to sell inferior products at inflated prices.

Each restaurant must have an "order bible." This should be an organized transcription from inventory onto a sturdy covered record book in which weekly orders are recorded with both listed prices and quoted prices. After an order is given, it is a good policy to have the salesperson look over the order to make sure that all of the quoted prices are correct. Once he or she has done this, he/she should initial it with the correct date. This will maintain an honest relationship between buyer and seller. This book should be kept in a place that is easily accessible when the order is delivered. The order bible should be checked against the delivery invoice at the time of delivery and once again when the invoice is filed. There should be notations about any discrepancies, and these should be brought to the attention of the salesperson the very moment he or she walks in to take the next order. Dramatic presentation of such facts can be quite effective.

The restaurant should not accept deliveries at restaurant prime times, such as noon to 1:30 p.m. or after 5 p.m. During these times your lot should be reserved for customer parking only. All personnel should be paying attention to customer service, rather than accepting deliveries and checking invoices. This may seem strict, but deliveries generally cause much more noise than is acceptable for a good dining atmosphere.

Delivery moratoriums should be clear to all suppliers. If there is a severe problem with this, contact the warehouse manager or the traffic manager at the wholesaling company with your complaint.

Telephone solicitations

I have always believed that buying over the phone is not a good way to get good product at good prices. Person-to-person buying keeps everyone honest. *Never* buy new products over the phone from an unknown salesperson.

If you order by phone, be extremely careful: most deliveries with inappropriate product or misquoted prices are the result of bad telephone communications. Too often, the wrong item is delivered at the wrong time with the wrong price. To avoid mistakes on phone orders, a form should be used that lists the following:

1. Name of company and time and date of order.

2. Name of person placing the order.

3. Name of the person with whom the order is being placed.

4. Brand name and prices of items.

5. Date and time of promised delivery.

When a restaurant is organized and asks a vendor for this information, one can generally expect a more accurate delivery. A vendor's phone receptionist is more likely to perform more efficiently when asked for his or her name along with other very specific information.

Keep them coming

Competition is the most important part of the buying equation. It insures quality goods at low prices. A medium-sized restaurant should always deal with at least three vendors who sell large-cost items such as meat, fish, groceries, and produce. You will get much lower overall prices using this approach than if you deal with only one vendor. Competition eliminates low balling and stiffens competition for quality, price, and service. Sometimes certain beers, wines, and liquors have only one vendor due to franchising. For the most part, though, food items are available through all vendors. Keep the salespeople coming and your buying efforts will be successful.

Small buyers can be good buyers

Large hotels have employees whose sole job is buying. In some restaurants, the food-and-beverage manager is also the buyer. In others, the head chef is the buyer. In small restaurants, the owner/cook does all the purchasing. Regardless of the size of the enterprise, the same purchasing principles must be used to enhance the probability of good profit. Buying power (which large organizations have) and good buying are not necessarily the same. One need only look to the Pentagon defense contract scandals to understand that purchasing can be corruptive. Keep it honest and keep your profits strong!

MAJOR NONFOOD PURCHASING

Insurance

Insurance companies are one of the most maligned private enterprise groups. They are constantly criticized by both politicians and the insured. For my part, I believe that if they were allowed to operate in a freer marketplace, competition would help drive rates down and everyone would be better off.

It is important to understand that insurers have sources of income that may not necessarily come directly from insurance premiums. At a time when their market investments were reaping high profits, they were almost giving away products such as fire insurance. The small premiums they were receiving were invested in financial instruments that were netting substantial returns. When investment markets disappeared, premiums tripled and there was an outcry about the high cost of insurance.

Shop around and get the best possible deals. The first task is to identify and list the restaurant's needs. Then you must set limits, so that your business is neither overinsured nor underinsured. Remember, restaurant insurance is value-based. So an evaluation of property, financial status, and catastrophic impact is pre-requisite to the purchase of a policy.

What is the total appraised value of the real estate? What is the total value of all other assets, including good will? How would a tragic event that injures a key employee affect the business? The answers to these questions will determine your coverage.

Property insurance has a direct relationship to the value of the real estate or goods being insured. The opposite of this concept is life insurance, where the value of the policy is related to the amount of premium. If someone buys a $10,000,000 life insurance policy, at the time of death the estate receives the full $10,000,000. On the other hand, if one buys a $10,000,000 property plan and something happens, the amount paid is only the appraised loss.

For example, if a restaurant burns to the ground, and the value of the building, equipment, and furnishings is estimated at $3,000,000, and the premiums paid justify a $10,000,000 plan, the insured would only get $3,000,000. (It is unlikely that this would happen, however. The agent would probably realize the imbalance and try to set a realistic premium for a policy.) The main point is that you only get a settlement for what is actually lost. Have an appraisal, and pay premiums according to the actual worth.

Many companies sell multi-peril packages; many comprehensive plans are written specifically for the food-service industry.

The following are recommended coverages:

1. Fire and catastrophic insurance for the entire restaurant property.

2. Insurance that will cover the cost of loss of business for the length of time it takes to rebuild and begin doing business again, by supplying salaries for key personnel, making mortgage payments, and paying start-up costs.

3. Liability insurance (inside and outside). This covers accidents to people in the building or on the premises, for which the restaurant may be liable. When estimating the coverage, add up the total assets, because this is what has to be covered.

4. Product liability insurance. This also protects the assets from suits due to injury, illness, or death as a result of eating or using the product.

5. Liquor liability insurance. This provides protection from suits that result from death or injury because of serving a person too much alcohol.

In my opinion, robbery, burglary, and sign insurance are not worth the cost. With creativity, a business can protect itself adequately against these losses.

Once you have an exact definition of the multiperil insurance needs, you should present your plan to as many companies as possible. Go with the lowest bid (providing the company does not have a reputation that is suspect).

Helpful hints

1. Any insurance proposal must be compared word for word with any other. Just say, "I want your proposal to match this one verbatim."

2. For health insurance, go with HMOs or any reasonable plan that doesn't involve tons of paperwork before they pay a claim. Restaurants should not have to deal with these issues. I prefer plans that require a business to pay a modest premium while the insurer does all the paperwork.

3. Worker's compensation insurance is mandated by law, and rates are usually state regulated. However, you can ask an agent whether his company offers rebates for a very clean record.

In short, list the needs of your establishment, and then shop around for the best insurance deals you can find.

Negotiating a lease

Most leases read as if they were written before the Magna Carta. It is imperative that a prospective restaurateur employ a lawyer to either write, help write, or assist in interpreting a realty contract. After all, a lease is one of a business's most important documents.

Location, square footage, and building condition determine the cost of rent. A lease defines payment of rent (amount, and specific payment date), and spells out areas of responsibility for the maintenance of the premises, such as taxes, insurance, and other services. To save money on legal fees, both parties should talk about all of the issues before getting lawyers involved in the lease arrangements.

Types of leases

The best lease agreement is a long-term contract (twenty years or more) at a fixed annual cost. I know of large retailing corporations with bottom lines that are very unimpressive, but that trade at a premium on the stock exchange due to the value of their long-term leases. A lease generally contains a subletting clause, which allows the lessee (renter) to rent out the property. Due to inflation, the cost of renting a business facility has doubled every ten years. If this trend continues, one could rent a property at $3000 a month for twenty years, and get over $6000 per month for the second ten years. This kind of arrangement is hard to come by, but a restaurateur should make a strong effort to negotiate for one. Five years should be the minimum length of a lease.

The most desirable restaurant leases are

1. Long-term, fixed-dollar leases for the length of the contract,

2. Five-year leases with an option for an additional five years at a specified increase, or

3. Five-year leases with an additional five years optional. Inflation determines the increase for the second five years.

There are leases that are based on a guaranteed monthly rate, plus a percentage of gross sales or net profit or both. Stay away from these kinds of arrangements. They allow other people to share in the profits from your work. I feel that a businessperson already has enough partners who take a percentage—the federal, state, and local governments.

Computer cash register

Price is always important when buying anything, but with a computerized cash register there are many considerations beyond dollars and cents. Look to the companies who have been making business machines *for retailers* for years. A big name computer maker does not necessarily make a computer that is the best one for restaurant use.

Equipment

Before putting kitchen equipment, fabrication, and installation out to bid, look at the cost of contracting with local firms. Those who can do their own contracting save about 30 percent, and it's not that hard to do.

Furniture

Shop around. Once, I conducted a nationwide search and finally had furniture shipped several hundred miles. The shipping costs were no problem: I still saved over 50 percent over the local outlets. Put in the effort, and the results will be rewarding.

8

RESTAURANT
FINANCES

8

RESTAURANT FINANCES

MONEY

MOST SMALL- TO MID-SIZE RESTAURANTS FAIL BECAUSE THE OWNERS or managers do not have an organized financial management system. A fiscal plan must begin with the understanding of money, and this understanding is rare. Money, while it is tangible, is the symbol for goods, services, activities, promises, and real estate. My accountant told me that some of the worst money managers are well-respected and cultured leaders of a community (doctors, lawyers, teachers, and city and town leaders). Intelligence and status do not necessarily translate into good money management.

When my wife and I were first out house shopping years ago, we were enthusiastic about a house that was a little over our heads. Every regional bank turned us down. We decided to try a cooperative bank located in a small town a few miles away from our home. A week after applying for the loan, I walked into the bank and asked if a decision had been made. The loan officer told me that the loan had been turned down, but the bank president was in the next office, and would I like to speak to him? The president told me that the loan was denied because, according to their analysis, my income was $50.00 a month too low. He said that our credit rating was good, but he felt we really couldn't afford that house. Half to myself, I said, "Well, that's only $12.50 a week that I'm short. If I could work four hours a week pumping gas, I could make up that deficit." The president immediately said, "Vincent, you just got yourself a new house and a twenty-year mortgage! Congratulations." He gave us the loan because he knew that I had an *understanding* of money. I didn't promise him that I would go out and get that gas station job. He simply gained confidence that I had the ability to subdivide and organize money into defined units in terms of income and expenditure.

Attitudes toward money

Money evokes funny attitudes in people. For example, if people read about a bank robbery in which the thieves get away with $300,000, they generally react with a host of contradictory concerns and emotions: fear that they might be held up and put at risk themselves; envy that the robbers might actually get away with all that cash; and a certain respect for the bravado of the robbers. However, if someone stole a $300,000 combination backhoe tractor, most people would simply wonder *why* anyone would steal a thing like that. In general, the backhoe thief would not get the same "respect" as the bank robbers.

There is a cliche that I have a tough time understanding; I hear it used by men and women living in every socioeconomic strata. It goes like this: "I'd better spend my money and enjoy it now, because I might be dead tomorrow." The fact is that most people live long lives, and their quality of life is directly related to financial stability.

Many people say that they want to get into the restaurant business because they like the cash flow. In most cases the direction of the flow is through a gaping hole in their pockets. Cash flow can be a great advantage when doing business, but there must be an organized plan to gain the benefits of having money readily accessible.

Joe the pocket

A good friend of mine ran a wonderful restaurant with much more volume than our place. Besides the disparity in the amount of business, our two establishments differed in another way. His business was constantly running behind in various payments, some of which were susceptible to heavy fines. But we had a system of check writing that left no leeway for late payments. He once asked me why my restaurant was in better financial shape than his. Knowing him as well as I did, and being aware of some of his tendencies, I asked him a few simple questions.

"Joe, how much business did you do yesterday?" "$10,000," he answered; "not bad for a Tuesday." Then I asked, "Where is the $10,000 right now?" "Well, you know, most of it probably got deposited this morning. Some had to go out for cash payments yesterday. We must have had some shortages. And Jane probably put quite a lot into petty cash!" Then I asked, "Joe, where's that nine iron you bought at Myrtle Beach?" He said, "Oh, that's in the front closet right between my two sets of clubs!" I smiled and said, "There's the difference between our restaurants, Joe. We did far less business than you, but I know that 2.73 percent was paid out in cash, 72 percent went into our payroll account and 3.71 percent went into petty cash. And I don't have any idea where my nine iron is!"

Every cent of a business must be accounted for. If money is carefully traced, the chances of a restaurant's success are greatly enhanced. If someone is responsible for $10,000, he's got to be able to account for all of it. What does that particular $10,000 actually represent?

Most people think of a specific amount of money and equate it to things that they want or places they travel to or future goals for their children. For example, $10,000 could translate into a 16 foot sailboat, a cruise for two to Hawaii, or college tuition. But if Joe wants to be a good money manager, he must recognize that $10,000 represents

1. that day's labor investment of his employees,

2. the goods that were consumed,

3. the cost of the facility for that day,

4. the taxes—federal, state or local—that were collected and are part of gross sales, and, last but not least,

5. the many patrons who came through the doors and actually spent the $10,000.

There are too many restaurateurs who do not look at the reality of the cash their establishment has generated.

If Joe appreciated the five points made above, his $10,000 would be divided up so that the appropriate funds could be set aside for payroll, cost of goods, maintenance, utilities, insurance, taxes and advertising.

Where's the profit for the owner? If all of this is done properly on a daily basis, the owner will be rewarded with a handsome profit. Once there is organization and money systems, the net result is legitimate profit. Remember, however, that profit is always the *bottom* line, after all other financial considerations. Every institution, individual, corporation, country, state, or city that is solvent, makes this kind of money management as one of its highest priorities.

Don the dropout

Gamblers are an interesting group. There are probably as many different kinds of gamblers as there are kinds of restaurant owners. As a youngster, I attended a parochial elementary school. One of my classmates, Don, who always sat in the back of the room, was barely passing from year to year. I remember that math was by far his weakest subject. By the time we were in the eighth grade, he had dropped out of school.

Years later, I met him at the racetrack. I noticed he had pencils behind both ears, was always writing and figuring, and would sometimes predict what a winning horse was going to pay. How did a grammar school dropout learn to calculate so quickly? I'm not sure, but I soon learned that he knew more practical math than I did.

He asked me if I knew what the rule of 72 was. I didn't and he soon gave me a clear definition. He told me that if I wanted to know how long it takes to double my money in the bank, take the number 72 and divide it by the interest rate and the answer is the number of years that it takes to double investments. For example, if one were to invest $10,000 at 12% interest, in six years one would have $20,000. The math is 72 divided by 12 equals 6. I've used this formula ever since to determine the place for my investments.

My former schoolmate was a professional gambler: he had to have a money management system. On the other hand, there *are* gamblers who have no system of money management; they are the big losers. In gambling, as in restaurant ownership, the losers outnumber the winners by a broad margin.

Good money management is not the rule in America. This may have something to do with the way we think about math in this country. In any event, control of one's financial destiny seems to be something that has to be learned. And for most people, gaining control requires changing some of their basic attitudes about money. But once you take an interest in the dollars and cents—as Don did—it really won't matter if you think you're "weak in math."

Trip to nowhere

I once asked a group of employees to write down five things they would do if I gave them $100,000 each. Most of the responses showed their benevolence, their caring, their needs and wants, and their tastes. But not one response showed any knowledge of money. There answers: "I would buy two tickets to Hawaii for my parents," "I would give my husband a new car," "I'd buy myself a brand new wardrobe." There was not one answer that took the future into account, or preservation of capital. If the person who wanted the trip for her parents were to invest the money properly, she could buy a trip *every year*, without touching the original $100,000. With practice, you can make progress toward these goals.

Financial responsibility is a matter of attitude, knowledge, and organization.

Debits and credits

In most manufacturing complexes the accounting involves

1. accounts payable, which is the payment or money owed to all of the suppliers and service companies, and

2. accounts receivable, the money or payments owed to the company for supplies and services rendered.

Unfortunately, in the restaurant business all you really have is accounts payable. You've already got the receivables in the cash register, and you better know what to do with them or you will not be able to deal with accounts payable.

The first questions I ask someone who is thinking of going into the restaurant business are, "What is your attitude toward money?" and, "What do you know about money management?" If the answers do not reflect concern for proper budgeting procedures, I tell the person to forget going into business independently, and use his talents as a faithful employee for someone else.

The cigar box theory

Terminology has changed, techniques have improved, and there is now more efficiency and better recording capability in business practices, but the basics of accounting have not changed since Shylock changed money in *The Merchant of Venice*! Accounting is still made up of categorizing financial information and then analyzing the results.

Many very small businessmen in the twenties, thirties and forties used cigar boxes to categorize receipts and payments. Each box held a different part of the basic budget. There was a box for rent, one for payroll, one for product, etc. The entrepreneur understood by previous analysis how much of each days receipts had to go into each box.

Did it work? Yes! Those who used the cigar boxes systematically (or similar devices) survived the depression. The unorganized shop and store owners went out of business. The cigar boxes were not only deposit chambers for bills to be paid and cash, they were also a means of storing information from which projections could be made, pricing could be updated, and net profit could be analyzed.

UNDERSTANDING FISCAL SYSTEMS

Accounting is important for every business, but the accounting procedures and terminology used by CPAs tend to be very complicated. Complete understanding requires the knowledge of a college graduate in accounting. Obviously, the restaurant manager, as proficient as he or she might be in fiscal matters, is unlikely to have all the knowledge to write a complete corporate financial statement. This is not the manager's job.

Accountants have developed standard accounting procedures specifically for restaurants; these basic standards are important in assessing profit and direction, and they also provide a restaurant with a respectable annual financial statement. However, a restaurant manager has a point of view that is affected by the daily, weekly, and monthly problems that occur, and that must be incorporated into any accounting scheme. These include

1. how to estimate the operating budget based on various types of expenses from fixed to flexible,

2. how to control the collection of money and its flow both internally and externally,

3. how to prioritize payments,

4. how to prioritize correspondence, and

5. how to properly assess profit and make sales projections.

Textbooks did not lead me to these conclusions. Rather, it was years of trial and error, and reactions to a real-life experience. In my case, several unpleasant episodes have inspired me to try to piece together a logical method of analyzing restaurant finances.

Who's paying?

I once had to help launch a restaurant for a large company. I was actually a subordinate of a much younger man who had graduated from one of the finest hospitality schools in the country. On the Saturday before the Monday that we were to submit a projected operating budget, I drove out to see him at his hotel. I wanted to voice my concerns on some work that I had done that indicated we were too low in our utility and insurance estimates.

He was, first and foremost, perturbed that I would bother him on a Saturday. I told him we were considerably off the mark, because we hadn't considered the square footage of the building. He looked at me and said, "I never include square footage in my estimates." I asked him, "Well, doesn't it cost more to heat, air condition, and clean a larger building than a smaller building? And isn't liability and fire insurance based on square footage?" He looked at me as if I had no knowledge whatsoever about budget concerns; he began talking in acronyms. He was going to give me a quick lesson in budget estimating.

I don't remember exactly what he said, but it was something like, "If you run everything through your B.O.B. and create an H.S. factor, the S.T.A. plus your S.T.D. should equal an F.D.P. That would put everything on line." Quite frankly, I was intimidated by his education, his articulation, and his arrogant, patronizing demeanor. I thought for a minute, slammed my hand down on the desk and said, "Look pal, I don't know what the hell you're talking about, and frankly at this moment I don't care. I do know it's going to cost over $3,000 a month to air condition that building, and we don't have it in the budget. All I want to know is, who is going to pay for it? Creative accounting?" We revised the budget.

Accounting procedures don't pay the bills; the restaurant does. The manager or owner is responsible for dealing with accounts payable and must have a clear understanding of what the costs are.

Estimating labor costs for the new restaurant

I once gave a projected payroll for a kitchen to a woman who I thought was a pretty good general manager. I took equipment costs and the square footage of the kitchen, and estimated what it would take to run that particular room through seven lunches and seven dinners per week. I presented a flat dollar amount based on the going hourly rates for kitchen staff in that locale. She looked at my work and said, "This isn't right. We don't figure labor costs according to dollar amounts, we figure it as a percentage of food sales." "Well, okay," I retorted. "Then it's 100% because this place won't be open for another month and that's the only time we'll know what the actual sales are."

The truth is, it is much easier to estimate basic labor costs if one analyzes the building, the equipment, and the basic kitchen chores, than it is to make sales projections for a new restaurant. Sales projections for a new restaurant are about as much of a guessing game as predicting the stock market.

Of salaries and accounting

For many of the larger restaurants that are part of large hotels, creative accounting removes the salaries of officers from the payroll assessment against the restaurant. If there were a prorata assessment, these large restaurants would reflect a much more gloomy picture when it comes to the bottom line. The general manager receives big pay, so why shouldn't at least part of the salary be considered a proportional share of the operating budget of the restaurant? I believe costs are shifted because the so-called experts don't want to show how bad they are at running restaurants. It's easy to absorb some of the restaurant expenses into the operating budget of the hotel. Too often, the main function of bureaucrats seems to be to solidify their own positions by using any means at their disposal to justify a department's existence, whether or not it is profitable.

It is common knowledge within the industry that hotel restaurants, by and large, do not pull their weight. Among the most recited excuses for this is the volatility of the restaurant business. The least recited excuse is poor management. The private entrepreneur with a restaurant as his only source of revenue does not have the luxury of hotel rooms to help bail out his establishment's inefficiencies. He's got to be profitable, or he's gone. Many hotels absorb much of their restaurant's expenses in the overall operating budget. These restaurants are not charged for square footage, or for lease, utilities, insurance, or maintenance. Incredibly, many of these restaurants still show a loss or break-even posture.

Projecting an operating budget for a restaurant that is not liable for basic operating costs would seem to be an easy task. For the self-contained or owner-operated establishment, the chore is much more difficult.

OPERATING BUDGET

When setting up an operating budget, the more predictable items should be dealt with at the beginning. There are some areas of budget planning that are fixed (rent, realty taxes, and fire insurance, for instance). On the other hand, there are some that are purely speculative, especially in new restaurants (such as food and beverage costs). As long as business continues to be competitive in a free market, there will always be a degree of volatility in the cost of doing business.

For a restaurant that has been in operation for a while, budget projections are fairly easy. There will be speculation about increases in product costs and general inflation, but the history of the restaurant will be helpful for projecting an accurate budget.

Fixed to flexible

An executive I once met with told me that projected sales for new products were almost always pure speculation. Long-range sales projections are as difficult to make as long-range weather predictions.

I owned a business on a street where a major fast food chain was building a new restaurant. I attended a meeting of 150 businesspeople from the community, sponsored by the firm. Company representatives told their whole story and assured everyone that they would be good and cooperative citizens. During the meeting, I learned they projected a total volume of $850,000 the first year. This was way off: as it turned out, they actually did $480,000 the first year. Not very good forecasting.

Sales projections seem to be the least predictable budget considerations. It's worth re-emphasizing that any budget forecasting should be done in order of relative predictability:

1. Fixed expenses that will not vary regardless of the volume.

2. Moderately predictable expenses, which can be defined within narrow limits.

3. Less predictable expenses, which are dependant on other dynamic factors but can be defined in broad parameters.

4. Flexible expenses, which are directly related to the amount of business or unforeseen events.

Following are grouped expenses and explanations of why they are in particular categories. This analysis assumes the restaurant for which the projections are made is new, and has no history for forecasting a budget.

Fixed expenses

(a) *Fixed leases and mortgages* should be documents that are written by attorneys or mortgage officers of banks. In either case the prospective restaurateur should retain legal counsel. Fixed leases require a definite dollar amount to be paid by the lessee on a periodic basis, usually monthly. The variables of such a lease might include insurance, maintenance, and tax increases. The definite, periodic dollar amount to be paid is stable and predictable on any forecast of expenses.

As we noted earlier, there are leases in which the payment can vary according to gross sales, gross profit, or net profit. The percentage payment is generally made on a quarterly, semiannual, or annual basis. These types of lease agreements add a degree of uncertainty for the budget analyzer. However, the fixed parts of these contracts are exact dollar amounts and have definite predictability.

When the restaurateur buys a building, the mortgage is generally paid in monthly installments. This should be absolutely predictable; it is bad policy for a business to enter into a mortgage arrangement that has a flexible or variable rate of interest. The restaurant owner should insist on a fixed rate of interest that he knows he can handle. He should not enter into any arrangement that makes him gamble on interest rate futures.

(b) *Liability insurance* rates are set by the insurer at a definite amount. This insurance protects the restaurant from suits brought by people who have been injured, either inside or outside of the building. The amount of the premium depends on the size and physical condition of the building.

(c) *Fire insurance* is a fixed premium. It is contingent on the building construction (wood frame, cement block, brick, or steel). Other factors that determine fire insurance premiums are sprinkler systems, fire-retardant drapes, proper fire walls and fire-blocking architecture, and kitchen fire extinguishing systems. Payments can be made annually, quarterly, or monthly and the premium is a definite dollar amount.

(d) *Realty taxes* are usually paid annually or biannually. They are a fixed yearly expense.

(e) *Accounting.* Both business and payroll accounting is usually on a defined and preset fee arrangement, or a service contract. (Do not enter into an hourly pay contract with an accountant.) Payroll service companies charge companies by the month at a very predictable rate.

(f) *Cleaning maintenance* companies have service contracts that spell out the job, the number of times per week or month each job will be done, and the exact dollar amount for each part of the service.

(g) *Exterminators* also have service contracts that are definite and can be included in the basic operating budget as a precise dollar amount.

(h) *License fees* are set by the local and state boards and do not vary within community limits. Most licenses are renewed annually.

(i) *Telephones.* Unless there is a great deal of long-distance calling, telephone bills are fairly easy to predict. A restaurant should have very limited expenses for out-of-town calls. Most types of communications are with the vendors, who generally pay for the long-distance fees.

(j) *Bank loans*, whether they are for equipment, beautification, or expansion, must always be taken out at a fixed rate of interest.

(k) *Bank fees* for checking accounts and other bank transactions should be negotiated with a bank officer so that they offer the best prospect for setting very narrow limits for these expenses.

Moderately predictable expenses

(a) *Health insurance* is related to payroll, and payroll usually is directly dependent on the volume of business. However, in the restaurant business, part-time employees (who are usually not covered), generally outnumber the full-time employees.

(b) *Electricity* use can be forecast by various means. One could canvas similar-sized restaurants and estimate according to the results. A more scientific approach requires knowledge of all equipment and lighting to be used. The forecast can be based on an analysis of consumption by kilowatt hour. Equipment manufacturers and distributors have a breakdown of approximately how much electricity it takes to run each piece of equipment for a specific amount of time. This is also true for lighting, both inside and outside. The local electric utility company and an electrician can be of service in evaluating future electrical expenses.

(c) *Gas* costs vary not only by usage, but also with the kind being used. Liquid propane is much more expensive than natural gas (which is not available where there are no gas lines under the streets). Gas utility companies have very sophisticated methods for analyzing equipment and projecting gas usage for most restaurants. They are a great source of information in estimating gas bills. Liquid propane vendors, manufacturers, and distributors of gas-using equipment can be similarly helpful in projecting those costs.

(d) *Water* bill estimates can be made with a call to the water utility company. Payments for water are generally made less frequently than payments for other utilities.

(e) *Heating* costs depend on many factors: the type of system, the energy source, the insulation factor, and the cubic feet of air space in the building. The different kinds of heating systems include forced hot air, forced hot water, and steam radiation. Sources of energy include oil, gas, electricity, or solar, singularly or in combination with each other. If the source is either gas or electricity, it has to be considered in its respective budget projection. If the heat is oil generated, a good boiler person can assist at arriving at an approximate fuel bill.

(f) *Equipment breakdowns* are usually covered by guarantees and warranties that accompany the purchase of new machinery. It's a good policy to purchase repair and maintenance contracts for much of the necessary equipment that is used on a daily basis. This helps the budgeting process.

(g) *Rubbish removal* bills usually depend on the cubic volume of trash generated by an establishment. The amount of rubbish determines the dumpster size. Fees are directly related to the size of the container and the number of pickups.

(h) *Office supplies.* Budgets can be made by using comparisons with other restaurants of similar size.

(i) *Paper supplies*, such as toilet paper and paper and wrapping products for take-out, can also be projected by comparing similar restaurants. Prospective suppliers will be happy to lend a helping hand.

(j) *The advertising budget.* This must be made up ahead of time, within known limits; that is, you must identify the minimum to be spent and the maximum. If the volume of business far exceeds expectations, it is wise to save the allotted funds for a rainy day. But the funds should still remain a part of the ad budget. If business is slower than expected, these monies should be allocated on the previously scheduled maximum use basis.

(k) *Maintenance* can be estimated by comparing with similar facilities. Don't be shy about asking around. You can introduce yourself and at the same time get some valuable information about your facility.

(l) *Snow removal* is, of course, influenced by the weather. However, restaurants that are located in parts of the country that receive a great deal of snow find that snow removal expenses don't vary much on a year-to-year basis.

Somewhat predictable

(a) *Payroll.* Labor costs are related to size of the facility, the menu, and ultimately to the volume of business. Therefore, payroll projections have some degree of certainty, because one knows the size of the building and the menu requirements. The unknown factor is the amount of trade that is going to be generated.

Question: Why aren't labor costs tied solely to the amount of business? Answer: Because the size of a facility and the type of fare are equally important.

For example, let's compare a 3000-square-foot room that does $10,000 to a 1000-square-foot room that does exactly the same amount of business. Wouldn't they require the same total payroll? The answer is no! The larger room would have more seating and, therefore, need more wait staff to cover the area of the room. The larger room also requires more kitchen personnel. For example, if the 1000-square-foot room were to fill up, it would take two line cooks to do the job properly. On the other hand, it would take five cooks to service a filled 3000-square-foot room adequately. One would have to keep five cooks even if the room filled up just once. (You can't have staff come into work for just one hour!)

The smaller establishment with the two line cooks can have two or three turnovers of tables, do as much volume as the larger facility, and properly service customers with a much smaller payroll.

Room size is crucial. Area and seating capacity are a factor in making valid payroll projections. A larger dining room *will* require more labor than a small one.

(b) *Kitchen payroll.* Understanding the type of menu can help you predict the amount of prep work required by the kitchen staff. A good budget predictor should ask:

1. Will we be using fresh homemade vegetables or canned products?

2. Will we be making our own soups?

3. How many frozen entree items are there?

4. How many house-prepared items are there?

5. How much work is involved in the preparation of all foods, and how labor intensive will the kitchen be?

Answers to these questions are extremely important in estimating the kitchen payroll.

The volume of business is directly related to labor costs, but for a new restaurant, sales are the unknown ingredient in budget projections.

In the mid-seventies, million-dollar restaurant chains such as Pizza Hut and The Ground Round, set a 22 percent labor cap as a goal. As the national economy improved, so did the percentage of labor costs as related to sales. If a restaurant has an anticipated sales figure, the payroll costs should be set at an ideal of 20-30 percent.

Training costs can range between 5-8 percent the first year of operation. Even though the minimum wage law is standard throughout the country, the cost of labor can vary greatly from region to region. The state and local government agencies can be of assistance in determining pay scales. If particular jobs are outlined and pay scales defined, a restaurant owner can predict his payroll within certain limits.

Less predictable expenses

(a) *Product liability insurance.* The premium for product liability insurance depends on the amount of insurance desired and the volume of business. Product liability insurance protects the restaurant owner in the event anyone has a claim against the establishment for injuries suffered due to consuming food or beverage products at the restaurant. For the middle-sized restaurant, a $1,000,000 policy is adequate. When a policy is underwritten the premium also depends on the projected amount of total sales. At some point after a restaurant has been in business, the insurance company will have the books audited and the amount of the premium may be adjusted based on the volume of business.

(b) *Liquor liability insurance* protects a restaurant from claims from anyone who is injured in an accident caused by a patron who has had too much to drink. A medium-sized facility usually needs about $1,000,000 of liquor liability insurance. The premium is based on the dollar amount of alcoholic beverages sold.

(c) *Worker's compensation insurance* is a mandatory protection for employee hospitalization or any medical costs that are a result of a job injury. It also protects the employee from loss of wages due to injuries that are job-related. Worker's Compensation is directly related to payroll; rates are usually set by the state. A restaurant's payroll is subject to audit by the insurer and generally, after the audit, the restaurant either owes or is owed money by the insurance company. Here the budget planner must work from the projected payroll.

(d) *Legal fees.* Allowance must be made for legal fees. A restaurant owner should enter into an arrangement with his lawyer for how much the fees will be and how fees will be paid.

(e) *Costs for linen supplies* depend on the amount of business. Generally, numbers of people— both customers and employees— determine how much linen is used. Linen companies can be very helpful with these projections.

(f) *Payroll taxes and surcharges* are based on payroll. Accountants can list the cost of payroll taxes and accompanying fees.

Projecting minimum gross sales

Food and beverage costs relate directly to sales. The difficult task is projecting a sales volume.

Traffic and demographics are all indicators that help project the dollar amount of sales. To predict traffic, poll similar restaurants in the vicinity; demographic projections can be obtained from government agencies. These dynamics are not absolutely reliable, and as we noted earlier, a lot of it is a guessing game.

Even in these seemingly pathless woods, there are land markers: known quantities that can help to determine the minimum amount of business needed to break even or to make a profit.

First one must arrive at an ideal percentage of total product cost as compared to total sales. Let's assume that the product cost should be 28 percent. The next task is to total all of the budget expenses, arrived at through the work done on budget forecasting. The sum of the projected basic expenses, plus 28 percent, will total the projected minimum gross needed to break even.

Let's assume further that the estimated operating budget is $453,000. Gross sales are 100 percent (gross sales are the whole, and the whole of something is always 100 percent). As we said, the ideal product cost was set at 28 percent. This tells us that the expenses are 72 percent (100 percent - 28 percent = 72 percent). So, $453,000 is 72 percent of gross sales. Using these numbers, we can calculate that the minimum amount of business necessary for survival is $629,166 over the first year.

The formula for the minimum amount of business needed to remain solvent is:

$$\frac{\text{PROJECTED OPERATING BUDGET}}{100\% - \text{IDEAL \% OF PRODUCT COSTS}} = \text{MINIMUM GROSS}$$

Anything above minimum gross is profit.

Projecting a dollar number for product costs requires simple math. Above it is 28 percent of gross, or $176,166.

If a restaurant has been in business for a year or more, forecasting becomes a little easier. However, one must not only rely on historical data, but also consider the direction of basic costs, the inflation rate, and any deterioration of the facility.

THE FLOW OF MONEY

The bank teller is behind a security barrier when transacting business. Supermarket cashiers are near the front of the store in line with cash registers. Fast food complexes have a defined point of sale. In all these settings, the flow of money can be traced: The customer enters the facility, makes a purchase, and makes a money transaction in a predictable way. The roles of both customer and service people are defined and almost always follow a set pattern.

In such environments, the accumulated money at the point of sale is periodically transferred to a safe or other secure place, where it is counted and usually made ready for a bank deposit. Since the money movement is so predictable, it is easy to draw a cash flow pattern:

In a restaurant, this kind of money flow is generally nonexistent. The manner in which the customer pays his check is not as defined as the manner in which someone checks out at a supermarket. On some checks, there may well be an instruction as to the method of payment, such as "Please pay the server" or "Please pay cashier," but usually the customer will use his own way of paying. He might take his check to the closest waiter or waitress, or signal the server and hand over the check and money, or walk over to the nearest cash register, or look for the right cash register, or signal a server, indicating that he has left both the check and the money on the table. Or he might do what I do—leave the check and money on the table and walk out without communicating with anyone. Customers are used to their own payment methods. It would be foolish to embark on a campaign to change these habits.

Easy money

There must be a clear and concise plan for cash accountability once the customer had paid. A restaurant is the only type of business I know of where it is common to see money unattended. It is usually seen lying on tables, on the bar, or on the waitstaff counters. Some of this money represents tips, some is payment for checks. Even cash register shortages are often overlooked by many restaurant owners and managers. In this loose-money atmosphere, employees must be instilled with an attitude of respect for money. The manager must bring order from the apparent chaos.

Server accountability

For over twenty years, I have been a strong advocate of making each server accountable for the cash of his or her total sales. Personnel who are tipped for food and beverage delivery and service are really in their own little business.

The expected tip is around 15 percent, and most waitstaff earn this or more. Their talents are contributing factors in how much they earn. The restaurant pays them a very small hourly wage, but a good waitperson can earn more than a food and beverage manager.

Waitstaff are usually given numbered checks for which they are responsible. Their cash totals must correspond to the totals on their checks. This is the reason I have always disagreed with the restaurant cashier concept, whether the cash register is behind the bar or near the exit to the serving area. These are situations where there are just too many hands in the till, and cash shortages are common. The server accountability concept does not allow for shortages. (See Fig. 20) Each waitperson is responsible for the total cash as shown in the total volume of business on his or her checks. This is explained in more detail later in the book.

WAITRESS TALLY SHEET

Cash Checks Paid _____

Master Charge _____

Voided Checks _____

Subtotal _____

Total _____

NAME

WAITRESS #   SHIFT: A   B

FIGURE 20

Proper cash register

Every restaurant should have a computerized point-of-sale cash register system. This type of unit usually pays for itself in six months. It consists of

1. A paneled keyboard, which has an entry for every item sold in the restaurant, along with appropriate identity features, such as "sirloin steak, well done," "baked pot.", "mixed veg."

2. A screen that shows the server the entry as it will be printed. This includes the cost of the item, the server's name and number and the number of the check. If several items are entered under a particular check number, the register stores a running total, to be charged along with the sales tax total and the sum total.

3. A check printer, which will list all of the items ordered for a particular check with corresponding prices, sum total for products and taxes, and the server name and number.

4. A kitchen printer, which informs the cooks of the food to prepare, with the name and number of the server and the time of day the entry was made.

5. A register tape that can print the volume of business for each server, the total business for the day, the volume and percentage of sales of each item on a daily, weekly, and monthly basis, and a running total of business from any given date.

This type of register avoids the staff's having to walk into the kitchen to place an order, eliminates the possibility of mistakes due to illegible handwriting, minimizes errors in totalling checks, saves time in servicing (since check totals are automatically calculated and printed at the time the order is placed), and gives the restaurant owner an accurate account of exactly what was ordered and the amount of cash that must be accounted for. (See Fig. 21)

OVERRING

DATE _____

OVERRING _____

REASON _____

INITIAL _____

FIGURE 21

Each server should have a cash box that can be locked, and is accessible only to waitstaff. The cash box should be big enough for cash and checks. At the end of the shift the waitperson totals up the checks and counts the cash to be turned over to the restaurant. The total money *must* be the same as the total printed by the register. This makes the server completely accountable for all money generated by his or her sales.

Let's assume that a waitress has counted the money; it equals her total on the register, and the corresponding checks are all in order. What next?

Money flow: From server to management to central money drop

The next step is very important in defining money flow for further accounting.

Many restaurants with good register systems (as described above) seem to lose the sense of good money flow after the server has accumulated and counted his or her cash. I have seen waitresses giving their money bags to bartenders, or food and beverage managers, or hostesses. In some restaurants in hotels, waitresses leave their receipts at the hotel desk or in the hotel office. Once money is in the hands of a middle person, a restaurant is asking for trouble and confusion.

In the restaurants I have been associated with, I have always insisted on the installation of a money bag drop system similar to those used for night deposits at a bank. It doesn't have to be as elaborate as a bank night depository, but it must be secure and its contents must be inaccessible to everyone except the manager or an accounting clerk. The best possible place for such a depository varies from restaurant to restaurant.

One might ask, "Why not just hand the money bag to the manager?" Human interactions are always dependent on many variables. A manager may be on the phone, talking to a customer, out of the building, or nowhere to be found. The depository removes all uncertainties. The server knows what to do with his or her receipts every time.

So far, we have followed money from the customer, to the waitress or waiter, to a central collection place. The next step is the reconciliation of all the funds for a particular day. If this procedure is done in the morning, the accounting is for the previous day's receipts. There should be a thorough count of receipts in each bag, compared to each server's totals. Any discrepancies should be handled as quickly as possible. (See Fig. 22)

VINNY'S RESTAURANT AND PIZZERIA, INC.

DAILY CASH REGISTER REPORT

FOR Y / E

DATE
REGISTER   #1 $
                    #2
                    #3 $_____

REGISTER ADJUSTMENTS:
Overcharges:

Cash to be Accounted for $_____

Less - Cash Paid Outs
(Total from detailed listing from other side) $_____

Total Amount to be Deposited $_____

Deposited Amounts $
                   Checking Account
                   Corporate Savings
                   Checking Account $_____

Total Amount Deposited $_____

Reason for discrepancies, if any, between amount to be deposited and actual deposited amount:

FIGURE 22

Dividing revenue

The manager, controller, or whoever is in charge of disbursing cash must divide the cash into appropriate units or accounts. I believe that every restaurant should have three bank accounts from which to make payments:

1. An account for payments to vendors, utilities, and most expenses that constitute the basic operating budget.

2. The payroll account, which also includes any payroll taxes.

3. A large expenditure account for mortgage, sales tax, and license payments.

Why not just one account? It is much easier to put the money into three predictable accounts and follow the funds in each category than to lump everything into one account. Payment systems are easier to manage. Payroll and payroll taxes should be a certain percentage of gross sales. If funds are allocated in a particular ratio, the ideal should be realized. For example, if payroll costs are 29 percent of gross, that percentage of daily receipts should be deposited in a payroll account. Like the cigar boxes of old, properly allocated monies are much easier to keep track of.

Large payments that are made monthly or quarterly, (such as mortgage or rent, insurance, sales tax or license fees) can be paid through an interest-bearing account such as a money market account. Sometimes the interest gained from such an account actually pays for one of the quarterly disbursements. Here again, the budgeting process determines the exact percentage of daily receipts that are deposited into such an account.

A determination of cash payments would help establish how much should be set aside beyond these categories. (See Fig. 23) The remainder, which would of course be 100 percent minus the percentages for payroll, money market and cash, would constitute the major checking account. If the system is administered properly the profit would be shown in the major checking account.

To the bank

Once the proper divisions of funding have been made and the correct entries have been written into a daily receipt ledger, the bank deposits should be made as early as possible. Bank balances for all accounts should be reconciled and recorded. At the end of the month average daily balances can be computed. If daily balances are large, lower banking fees can be negotiated through the bank manager. The management of the money flow from customer to server to central

TONY'S RESTAURANT AND PIZZERIA, INC.

SCHEDULE OF CASH PAID OUTS

DATE:

	VENDOR	TOTAL AMOUNT	MEATS & GROCERIES	PAPER SUPPLIES	STORE SUPPLIES	OTHER	
						DESCRIP.	AMOUNT

FIGURE 23

accounting area to the proper accounts is important for the financial stability of a restaurant.

Credit card payments delay the full realization of the bank balance, since money transfers are not finalized for three days to a week. One of the things I have learned through the years is that bank charges for credit card services are negotiable. This is an important consideration for a restaurant whose receipts are loaded with credit slips. The rates for services can range from 2 percent to 6 percent. Remember that the rate the restaurant pays applies to the total charged, including product charge, taxes, and tips. The total amount charged against the account could be substantial.

Basic bookkeeping

The restaurant office must have a basic journal on which entries can be made on a daily basis. This bookkeeping record should include a listing of receipts from each shift (breakfast, lunch, dinner, or evening), identified with corresponding rooms (dining room, cafe, lounge, or take-out), and a total of all receipts for that day. There should be a cash report entry detailing cash at opening, specified cash payments, and the closing cash balance inclusive of additional funds. If all deposits are made correctly and bookkeeping is done faithfully every day, a manager will have complete accountability of all receipts.

Every certified public accountant has his own method, forms, and procedures that he can install in a restaurant to obtain the necessary information he needs (filling out federal, state and local forms). He also makes up a financial statement—an analysis of the fiscal activities of a restaurant. He will summarize the accounting policies, figure out the method of depreciation, and calculate any taxes owned or overpaid. The only way an accountant can do this job properly is with access to all of the receipts and properly categorized disbursements that were transacted over a defined period of time. Besides governmental agencies, financial statements can be of interest to banks, insurers, and prospective buyers. The financial statement is an important document, and the accountant needs the restaurant's help in compiling the data.

During the check writing process, the number, payee, and categories of payment must be properly entered and carried out to an appropriate grouping where the type of disbursement can be easily identified (utility, loan, product, service, advertising, tax, repair, and so on). These groups have a bearing on the amount of taxes to be paid. All check payments must be subtracted and all deposits must be listed and added to the carrying bank balance.

Neglecting to reconcile bank statements is a disease that runs rampant in many American households. This sickness can be terminal for restaurants, especially if someone has the ability to compromise the checking system. Reconciliation of cancelled checks to bank statements should be accomplished on the date the bank statement is received.

Systems for payments and filing invoices

Every office or business should have a filing system so that the controller or bill payer can readily identify whether or not bills have been paid. This is usually accomplished by having a designated place in the files to distinguish paid from unpaid invoices. Paid invoices can be stamped or marked appropriately with the date, method of payment (cash or check, with number), signature of person making the payment, whether it was delivered by mail or in person, and the signature of the receiver of the payment. The paid invoices should then be placed in the file folder according to date. Some restaurants have two sets of files and two sets of file folders, one for paid invoices, the other for unpaid invoices.

My system involves two sets of files, paid and unpaid, but only the paid file is company specific. The unpaid file is organized by the days of the month. There are two secrets to this system. One is that every bill, invoice, or statement is marked with the date of delivery and desired date of payment. The second is that there are a maximum of thirty-one days in any given month. Therefore, the unpaid file is limited to thirty-one folders, since there are only thirty-one possible days in a month to make disbursements.

The paid file is opened and used when the newly paid invoices are placed in it and to confirm payment in the event there is a question from a supplier. It is a bulky and cumbersome file drawer, but it should get very little use. There are hundreds of folders in this file, but only thirty-one in the unpaid file, which is the most used.

Let's assume that it is Wednesday, June 25. At the restaurant, there have been five deliveries with accompanying invoices. Several bills have been received through the mail, and statements, bills, and invoices are now ready for filing. Among them are an electric bill and a water bill. The due dates are on all of the statements, but the filer only has to worry about the day of the month and ignores the actual month on the invoice. Let's say that the due date on the electric bill is July 10. The filer can place that invoice in the folder marked 8, to allow time for mailing. Let's assume that the water bill is due August 15. Again, he or she need not be concerned about the month. The filer places that invoice in folder 13, again leaving some time for postal dispatch. All other statements or invoices can be placed in the file according to due day. If it is organized properly, this work can be done in less than five minutes per day.

Actual disbursements

How does this system work when making payments? Let's look at another hypothetical situation. It is Monday, June 30. All work has been done in terms of reconciling receipts, and the bank deposits have been made. It is now time to deal with accounts payable. These are the steps to follow.

1. Take out the folder marked 30 from the file. Since it is Monday and nothing was paid out over the weekend, also remove the folders marked 28 and 29, in the event there was an error in filing. If the filing was done with consideration for the weekend, invoices filed for the 28 and 29th should have been in folder 27. (The filer should work according to a calendar.)

2. Go through all of the invoices and statements to make sure the due dates are relative to June 28, 29 or 30. Let's assume one of them is an excise tax bill marked September 2; put it back in the folder marked 30 (again, allowing for mailing time).

3. Make out the appropriate checks, with the corresponding invoice number included. Mark the invoice as paid, and write in the check number, date mailed, and your signature.

4. Place paid invoices in the paid file in the correct folders.

This system works. There are almost no costly fines and many opportunities for discounts. Those restaurants with computers can use the same basic system and take advantage of electronic recording of the vital information. If a restaurant is dealing with 150 accounts payable, instead of keeping track of 300 folders, the bookkeeper is dealing with only 181. Out of those only 31 contain the information pertaining to accounts payable.

REASON FOR PRIORITY DISBURSEMENTS

A restaurant that is run properly should not be behind in any of its obligations. Accounts payable should be made right on time. However, I believe that a manager should have a list of payments that must take priority over others. Some late payments bear heavy fines and some early payments are rewarded with discounts. In the event an establishment should run into a period of financial difficulties, a manager must categorize the bills as follows:

1. Those that affect the continuation of business.

2. Those whose payments can be delayed to a degree.

3. Those whose payments can be delayed for longer periods of time.

People to pay first

By far the most costly late payment charges are made by the tax collecting agencies of the federal and state government. They will charge a fine plus interest, and interest on both if there are long delays in payment. A $2,000 charge can become $4,000 in a relatively short time. These agencies are unrelenting and are the first to close a restaurant for nonpayment. Local taxes of all kinds are top priority payments, for it is the local governing boards who issue all of the necessary licenses and permits. A priority should be placed on prompt payment for all licenses. Sometimes, when license fees are not paid on time, local boards insist that restaurants reapply. If the liquor license is the one in question, the application process could take quite some time.

Electric bills should be paid promptly for two reasons:

1. Late payments can result in the cutting off of services.

2. Many electric power companies reward punctual payments with discounts of up to 10 percent. The savings for larger restaurants can be in the thousands of dollars.

Gas companies have been known to cut off the services that they supply after a couple of months of nonpayment. Sometimes they will not restore the service unless the user makes a large deposit. Telephone companies, similarly, don't hesitate in shutting down the communication capabilities of a facility if there is a payment problem. Heating bills, too, should be paid promptly.

There are late payment penalties for mortgages: lending institutions are less patient than they were in the fifties and sixties. There have been many bank failures, and banks have placed restaurants on the top of the list of those least likely to repay debts. They move quickly when a restaurant is late making payments.

All insurance policies are, in effect, a protection of the assets of the restaurant. The associated premiums should be paid on time. I know of a restaurant that was behind in its health insurance payments; an employee was stricken at home, and required an operation and two weeks of hospitalization. In the meantime, the insurance was cancelled. This incident cost the restaurant $28,000.

Some insurance policies may be cancelled with one notification, while others may be cancelled on a defined timetable, with notification by a registered letter. Insurance laws differ from state to state; you should understand how billing and cancellation notices are mandated for your restaurant.

All of the items listed above must be paid promptly in order to maintain the solvency of the business. In our restaurants, we have a list of all these essential payments in large print on wall posters. Printed next to the item is the method and day of payment.

The priority list is not intended as a system of chronological payments, but rather as a tool to magnify the importance of particular payments.

Payments that can be delayed

If one person owes another person money, the worst scenario for both parties is the death of the debtor. Likewise, most vendors who are owed money by a restaurant will not want to see a bankruptcy. If an establishment gets into financial difficulties, the manager should make a list of all companies that are owed money and appeal for a payment schedule that allows for certain deferments. For example, he can call the rubbish collector and ask for a delay of fifteen to thirty days in the billing process. Generally, a vendor will not be thrilled by a delay in compensation, but accept it; he really has no other choice.

Most vendors are used to chasing money, and often run into debtors who can't be reached by phone, make promises that are untrue (like "the check's in the mail"), or conveniently change vendors as soon as money is owed. A forthright statement with an appeal for some mercy is refreshing to both product and service vendors.

Those companies who might work with a restaurant in trouble include electricians, air conditioning specialists, plumbers, paper suppliers, equipment repair services, banks, maintenance and cleaning specialists, advertising and media services, accountants, lawyers, and septic cleaners.

Bills you can delay the most

Any business whose credit rating is low must understand that it has lost much of its leverage in dealing with suppliers. The purchasing session with salespeople is now dedicated to methods of payments rather than achieving good prices for the restaurant. It is in the best interest of a business to make every effort to avoid situations of indebtedness.

It is no secret that if a restaurant fails, major suppliers have the most to lose. They have a vested interest in the survival of the business. If bankruptcy occurs, they are the last ones to share in the remaining equity and usually lose everything they have claim to. Most large food suppliers understand that if a restaurant does not pay the tax collector, the collector will shut down the business and lay claim to assets immediately. A restaurant in such difficulty can work with large food distributors. Ordinarily, suppliers will ship orders on a C.O.D. basis, hoping the establishment will eventually bail out and start paying past-due invoices.

Liquor distributors have payment schedules from thirty to sixty days. In some states, when these bills become overdue, the establishment is reported to a state agency and all alcoholic beverages must be paid for on a C.O.D. basis. In the industry, this is called "being on the list." I have seen situations where restaurants were unable to pay for liquor deliveries on a C.O.D. basis and had to resort to buying single bottles at liquor stores. This, of course, does not help profit margins.

Bad reputation is one of the most damaging results of delayed bill-paying policies. Pay your bills on time, and you will have a smooth operation.

Priority correspondence

Most companies separate their mail according to importance. There is always a stack of very significant correspondence, less significant mail, and wastebasket material. In larger companies, various departments make their own categories of significant mail. In a small business the significance of each piece of correspondence is much more difficult to ascertain.

At times, if the importance of a letter is not understood, the result can be the loss of a necessary license, the loss of desired credit, or the payment of unnecessary fines or interest. Most of the critical mailings that come under this classification are sent by government agencies, the courts, or insurance companies.

Due to the consequences that can result from delayed reaction or misunderstanding, I recommend a Priority Mail List to be posted in broad lettering in the office. This tells the origin of the correspondence and what to do once a letter of this nature is received. For example, "Mailing from the I.R.S., make a copy and call Bob Johnson, Accountant, Tel. 829-9734."

This takes the guesswork away from both staff and management. Much correspondence for chartered institutions is difficult to understand and should be left up to the professionals for interpretation.

In 1987, a questionnaire that was mandated by a state Alcoholic Beverage Commission had a response deadline of November 1. On this correspondence there were several clues that indicated its importance. One was that questions had to be answered and mailed to the licensing board by November or there would have to be a reapplication procedure for a new license. The other was a place for the signature of the owner or manager under penalties of perjury. The questionnaire's purpose was, in effect, to find out if all liquor taxes had been accounted for.

I know of one restaurant that did not comply. It was not licensed by January and had to reapply for a liquor license. Unfortunately, this time around the local licensing board (which was not part of the inquiry) was not as friendly as it had been when the license was first granted.

The establishment eventually was awarded a new liquor license, but at great expense in terms of both loss of business and unnecessary expenditures. The irony is that the intent of the questionnaire was to weed out the restaurants that didn't pay liquor sales taxes. This restaurant was solid in that regard, but suffered due to an unorganized correspondence system.

Important correspondence can be difficult to separate from less important mailings. Therefore, I believe a priority list is vital and should be in view of all office staff. A suggested model for such a list includes

1. Any correspondence related to taxes—contact the accountant.

2. Anything received from any government body—contact the attorney.

3. Any correspondence from courts, sheriff's office, police, other attorney—contact the attorney.

4. Any letters from actual insurers
   (a) contact insurance agent;
   (b) forward copy to the attorney.

Your communications on the above matters are important to the financial stability of your restaurant.

ASSESSING PROFIT

Many of us look at wealth in terms of the exterior, or what is obvious on the surface. All of us have heard things like, "The guy's loaded. He owns a Jaguar, a big house in Maine, a house in Florida, a condo in Vegas, and his wife is overweight because of the jewelry." I always question whether this wealth is just skin deep.

What is the ratio of his debt to equity? That is the real measure of financial worth. If he owes more than he has or will ever earn, he's actually poor.

Some restaurant practices make profit hard to appraise. Unfortunately, some owners do not make a distinction between themselves and the business. Owner and establishment are two separate entities. Much of my consulting work is spent trying to convince restaurant owners of this reality. The proprietor owns the restaurant, but he *is not* the restaurant. Comingling his funds with the funds of the establishment is a serious mistake he will regret making.

An owner or manager does not have the right to take money from the cash register without being accountable for it. This is against the law. Why? Let's assume an owner takes $50 from the cash register and spends it at the racetrack. If he did not record that expenditure in the restaurant books, the $50 is unaccounted for, and the IRS would certainly not condone the situation. Technically, the $50 should be reported as income.

The big shot who "sets up the bar" must have the "clams" in his pocket to pay for the drinks. This owner or manager rarely pays for anything. When a manager is blase about the relationship between products and profit and the rigid accountability of both, his attitude can spread like a disease.

Whenever I have entered one of my own establishments, I play one of two roles.

1. Manager—I work!

2. Customer—I pay!

Don't cheat on taxes

In the classified ads, I have read, "Restaurant for sale—Reported Gross Is . . ." This must mean that there is unreported gross or two sets of books. Any restaurant manager who underreports earnings to avoid taxes does not understand equity and is cheating himself. A formula that is frequently used to estimate the selling price of a profitable food establishment is that the value of a restaurant equals one half of the yearly average of gross business for the last three years (not including the building).

Let's assume that a restaurant does not report $100,000 of its earnings to avoid a 5 percent sales tax. Over a one-year period, it saves $5,000 in cash, but loses $50,000 in equity. If someone wanted to buy the restaurant, the owner would have to sell it for $50,000 under its true value. Besides, tax evasion is illegal and punishable by imprisonment.

Make a list of your taxes and when they are due. Post it in your office. Remember, a restaurant would have to cheat for ten years in order to approximate one year's loss in equity. The kind of restaurant owner who cheats in this way generally will have nothing to show for his efforts after ten years. If a food enterprise is run properly and aboveboard, a manager can readily assess its profitability.

How to figure out profit

In order to know the gross or net profit, a business must have a specific fiscal year: a twelve-month period commencing on the month that the business first opened. For the purpose of worthwhile analysis, the fiscal year must be divided into fiscal quarters and weeks. The fiscal week must begin on the day inventory is taken and end the night before. If inventory is done on a Monday morning, the week must run from Monday through Sunday. This is logical for a restaurant, because Sunday is considered part of the weekend. If the fiscal week is set up properly, an exact correlation between sales, product, and inventory will result.

Defining a month is a little more difficult. In each three- month period there will be 13 weeks. One month will have 5 weeks and two months will have 4 weeks. In order to bring clarity to this process, I suggest a fiscal calendar. This can be put together very easily on a large poster. It will be up to the management to decide which months will have five weeks. Once there are defined fiscal weeks and months, the manager can obtain a true analysis of the financial condition of the establishment.

Put simply, net profit is what is earned minus what is spent. Because some major restaurant expenses are paid in lump sums, the true impact of these payments must be pro-rated over twelve months to determine their actual effect. In a small restaurant the writing of a financial statement is a once-a-year event. Still, the owner or manager should have a monthly fiscal evaluation. In order to gain this data, the owner must gather and organize specific information relative to a defined time (the first day of the month to the last day of the month). He/she needs this information to arrive at the gross profit, the total sales minus the cost of sales. For this the manager must compile the following:

1. total gross sales for the month,

2. total payroll for the month,

3. inventories at the beginning of the month,

4. inventories at the end of the month, and

5. total cost of food received for the month. (Not necessarily paid invoices, just goods received.)

Next, one must reconcile the inventory and apply the difference to the cost of food (plus or minus). For example, if the inventory lists five sirloins at the beginning of the month and four at the end of the month, the conclusion is that the establishment had used one more sirloin than it received. Therefore, the cost of one sirloin has to be added to the cost of sirloins received. If the average price of sirloins for the month is $3.75 per pound, and a sirloin weighs 12 pounds, $45 has to be added to the net cost of food. The opposite is true if inventory showed four sirloins at the beginning of the month and five at the end. In this case, $45 is deducted from the net cost of food.

The net cost of food is the total cost of food received, minus or plus the value of the inventory differential. The result is the actual cost of food sold. Cost of food plus cost of payroll equals the cost of sales, and sales minus the cost of sales equals the gross profit. The next task is to get a monthly average of all other operating expenses. This can be compiled by reviewing historical data and by obtaining the numbers from the projected operating expenses.

The gross profit minus other operating expenses equals the net profit. The net profit gives the restaurant owner a clear idea of the profit the establishment is actually earning.

```
   Sales
 — Cost of sales (product and labor) or prime cost
 = Gross profit
 — Operating expenses
 _____
 = Net profit
```

Side benefits of fiscal evaluation

Other important information can be gained by a precise evaluation of sales and costs. A manager can see if the actual cost to sales conforms to the original outline that was assembled during menu planning. If the menu and specs were designed to result in 70 percent gross return, certain questions will arise. Are goals being met? Are costs too high? Do percentages of profits exceed expectations? Are they right in line? All of these questions can be answered by analyzing the numbers and results in the analysis of gross profit. To find out the percentage of product cost to sales, divide the net cost of product by the gross sales. For example, $13,000 product cost divided by $40,000 gross sales equals 32.5 percent. This same formula can be used to evaluate food, beverage, and payroll cost.

An informed manager can have an effect when communicating with anyone in the organization. If he has an accurate analysis and tells the chef that food costs are too high, he's not guessing. He has facts and figures to back up the claim.

A FEW WORDS ON SALES GOALS

Once a restaurant has a business history of one or more fiscal years, a sales projection must include a reflection of the forecasted inflation rate, plus a desired growth rate for the establishment. As the saying goes, "You can't stand still or you'll go backwards." Anyone who wants to accomplish something must set goals that are reasonable but not easily attainable. If a restaurant has total sales of $863,498, and the inflation rate is forecasted at 5 percent, and if management decides that in order to achieve a better bottom line, it will be necessary to do 10 percent more business, then the next year's sales total has to rise to $997,339. ($863,498 + 5% inflation = $906,672 + 10% desired increase in business = $997,339.) That means the restaurant has to average $83,111 per month. Since some months are slower than others, the forecaster must adjust the projections seasonally. Busy seasons vary according to location.

A graph is a useful tool both for making projections and understanding whether the actual business totals correlate to the goals. One can make a graph with a fifty-two week schedule based on the restaurant's fiscal year. This will be a visual representation of the set goals and actual goals. Such a graph is just another means of putting management in touch with the reality of the financial ends of the business. (See Fig. 24)

PROJECTION—Desired sales $1,000,000 ($19,230 weekly)

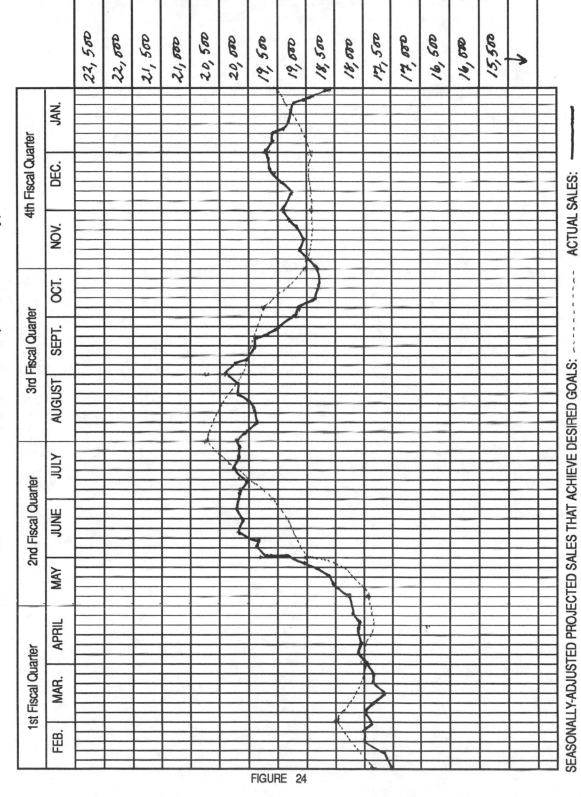

		1st Fiscal Quarter		2nd Fiscal Quarter			3rd Fiscal Quarter			4th Fiscal Quarter		
FEB.	MAR.	APRIL	MAY	JUNE	JULY	AUGUST	SEPT.	OCT.	NOV.	DEC.	JAN.	

22,500
22,000
21,500
21,000
20,500
20,000
19,500
19,000
18,500
18,000
17,500
17,000
16,500
16,000
15,500

FIGURE 24

SEASONALLY-ADJUSTED PROJECTED SALES THAT ACHIEVE DESIRED GOALS: - - - - - - - - ACTUAL SALES: ————

9

**FACILITY
MANAGEMENT**

9

FACILITY MANAGEMENT

UNDERSTANDING THE BUILDING

RESTAURANTS ARE VULNERABLE TO CRITICISM FROM PUBLIC SAFETY and public health officials on the issue of facility management. Unfortunately, many managers don't fully understand this. They give very little consideration to the structure in which the business exists.

A chain that had all of its outlets in the inner city decided to expand into the suburbs. At the city locations, sewer pipes leaving their buildings ran along heated chambers, so employees emptied the deep-fat fryer grease directly into the drain system. Because the grease was hot when it was emptied, it did not solidify until it was safely into the sewer system.

In their first suburban restaurant, the same system of grease disposal was a disaster. The grease solidified within a few minutes. All of the drains backup up, and it took a drain-cleaning company two days to clean all of the pipes.

The net result was the loss of the weekend business, the cost of cleanup, angry patrons who had made reservations only to be turned away at the door, and most of all, tremendous damage to the restaurant's reputation.

There have been restaurant horror stories of repair people being called for a specific problem and hanging around the establishment for hours: the person who called never gave the instructions necessary for someone to direct the repair person to the exact problem. Most companies start charging for their services once the craftsman *leaves for the job*. Remember, too, that a restaurant at its peak business hours can be a confusing place for any repairperson. The management must set up guidelines that allow technicians to enter and service problems expeditiously.

Location can determine the kind of equipment, energy sources, and waste disposal systems needed for operation. Gas, oil, water, and electricity sources can vary and they do affect both the equipment and the facility. (Some buildings, for instance, are not located on a natural-gas line.)

A large hotel I worked at was built in a mountain resort many miles from natural gas. The restaurant inside had done extensive advertising and was to open on a weekend. It had a dining facility with a very ambitious menu. The equipment was hooked up and ready to go, but when employees tried to light the pilots for their burners, none of them would light. They had neglected to adapt their equipment from natural gas to the liquid propane that fed this building! This error was management's fault. Management either hired the wrong vendors or didn't follow up on equipment research.

The general manager of a large hotel told me about some of the problems they had when the hotel was brand new. They hired a new purchasing agent who was anxious to show how he could save money. He bought all of the tile for the kitchen and restroom floors from an international tile company. After installation, one of the main comments from people walking through the building was that the tile looked beautiful. The one person who didn't agree with this description was the chef. He complained that no one would be able to work on the floor because it would be too slippery: it was a glazed tile and in no way appropriate for a kitchen. The initial savings in the cost of the tile was more than offset by the cost of installing nonskid strips over the floor.

These are incidents that actually happened to larger companies. Most companies have the resources to avoid these embarrassments, but money does not always translate into effective management.

WHAT A MANAGER SHOULD KNOW

Knowledge of the physical plant can help you avoid unnecessary closings, spoilage (in the event refrigeration is down), inflated repair costs, unnecessary repair costs, and liability suits.

There should be an architectural plan of the building accessible to repair people. Drawings should be made that locate and identify the equipment in each system. These should include:

1. A map detailing the location of all compressors, fans, and condensors used for refrigeration and air conditioning.

2. A plan that shows the major outlets, switches, ballasts, break panels, the power entry location, and the electrical meter.

3. A schematic drawing of major drains and drain pipes, along with the exiting location of the major waste conduit and grease trap.

4. A drawing showing the entrance of the water supply and the kind of supply (such as two-inch service or six-inch service for restaurants that have sprinkler systems). This drawing should include sinks, faucets, and dishwashers.

5. The location of the gas shutoffs. There are safety concerns with any kind of power, but gas leaks or a broken burner part can be exceptionally dangerous.

6. Access to boiler rooms, cellars, and attic entrances.

A manager should not be required to have the same knowledge as a custodial engineer. But armed with *some* knowledge, the manager can minimize repair costs. If there is a problem with a piece of equipment, it is an advantage to know exactly what the problem is. If a walk-in refrigerator is not working, the first step is to try to isolate the problem prior to calling the repair company. Generally, when no knowledge is offered, the repair person come in, see what the problem is, and then leave to pick up the appropriate part.

If one knows that the problem is with the fan, the repairperson will ask you to check fuses to eliminate some possibilities. If the problem is a breaker or fuse, repair costs can be totally eliminated.

The repairperson might ask you for a model number. Providing this information might save the time it takes to come to the restaurant, write down a model number, and go pick up the part. Learn to communicate with your service repair people. They will respect you and will save you time and money.

We had a huge oven in one restaurant I worked in. The oven went out, so we called the local utility company to find the out what problem was. They showed up in no more than half an hour after we called them. After a short analysis of the problem, they told us that a burned out heat reflector had cause the pilot to shut off. They didn't have the part in stock; it would have to be ordered from the manufacturer. They had to go through the bureaucracy of a large utility to obtain an enumerated, authorized purchase order and then mail it to the manufacturer in Burlington, Vermont. Estimated down time: five days to two weeks.

This was our main oven. We couldn't wait two weeks. We called the manufacturer and asked if we could drive in and pick up the part. They said fine, but noted that they would not be open after 5:00 p.m. It was already 3:00 p.m. when we called; this meant the oven would not be fixed for dinner that night or for the following day's lunch, since the office would not open until 8:00 a.m. Even an overnight ride wouldn't help. Then I got an idea.

I called the manufacturer again, asked them to call a cab, put the package on the 4:35 p.m. Peter Pan bus to Springfield, Massachusetts, and C.O.D. the package, including cab fare, all the way to Worcester (where we were). Noting my determination and believing they could trust me, the manufacturer said they would pay the transport fees and bill me later. I called the gas company and asked if I could have a repairman at the restaurant first thing in the morning. They agreed. At ten that evening, I picked up the reflector at the bus terminal in Worcester. The next day we had a relaxed and profitable lunch hour at the restaurant. The total transportation cost: $35.00.

PREVENTIVE MAINTENANCE

One of the keys to insuring a well-run facility is preventive maintenance. The management should encourage employees to try to recognize and report equipment that seems to be deteriorating. The wallpaper in the dining room , for instance, could be changing color because of a problem on the roof. If the problem is structural, its worsening could pose a real danger.

The worst kind of publicity for a business is a newspaper, radio, or television report that someone got hurt at the establishment. This is one very good reason a manager should get into the habit of listening to employees' reports of facility breakdowns.

I once heard about a chef who told his superior that a flexible electric conduit in the walk-in refrigerator was hanging a little more than usual. His warnings went unheeded, and the situation kept worsening. Even when the chef gave more warnings there was no effort made to solve the problem; the manager showed little concern. One day, a youngster was sent to the walk-in to get some produce. When he opened the door, the light went out but the fan kept running.

The youngster felt around in the dark and accidently touched the conduit. He received a bad shock and the circuit blew, shutting down the walk-in. The breaker would not go on, so an electrician was called to rewire the conduit. This incident caused much more heartache than cost of the electrician, the kitchen losing efficiency for two hours, or the possibility of spoilage. The youngster was scared badly and went home to tell his father, who was in the fire department. Monday morning, every inspector in the city was at the restaurant combing the building, and making recommendations, some of which were very costly to the restaurant. The cost of the ill will created by this type of incident is much steeper—and completely avoidable.

In another instance, at a different restaurant, a wooden platform that led to the dumpster area had been slowly decaying for some time. A dishwasher went out to empty the trash; one leg went through the platform. This youngster had to be brought to the emergency ward of the local hospital. The restaurant had to pay worker's compensation, the parents filed a liability suit, inspectors closed the restaurant until proper repairs could be made, business was lost, and the restaurant received a great deal of bad publicity. All of this could have been avoided by repairing that platform which would have cost less than $70.00.

Do not place building maintenance low on the priority list. A facility that is not properly maintained can result in serious injury to customers and/or employees. Needless to say, this could lead to the demise of the restaurant and a negligence suit against the management.

Upkeep of the grounds is equally important. If a person is seriously hurt tripping in a hole in the parking lot, the lawsuit can be substantial. Lack of concern for maintenance risks *all* your assets.

HIRING SERVICE PERSONNEL

In the chapter on purchasing, I emphasized having enough vendors to encourage competition. This might not be advantageous when purchasing the services of maintenance experts. While price should be a factor in determining your electrician, there are other very important consideration, including:

1. Does the electrician have the expertise to service your building and all of your equipment?

2. Does the electrician work hours that are compatible with your business?

3. Does the electrician have a staff big enough to respond quickly to emergencies?

4. Does the electrician have an efficient telephone system, so that an emergency call can be put through quickly?

5. Is the electrician close enough to minimize travel time?

The best service contractor for any facility is the one that can readily respond to your needs. The contractor must have an appropriate license to work in a public building, of course. A good technician can save breakdown costs, excessive utility costs, and equipment replacement costs.

A refrigeration mechanic once told me to put all compressors into a specified area away from the refrigerators themselves. Compressors create heat that warms the exterior walls of the refrigerator. When the refrigerator door is opened, the warm air flows into the unit. In effect, compressors have to work hard just to cool off the hot air they generate. This is a mad cycle that costs energy and money. By putting all of the compressors in one place away from the kitchen, one can recapture the heat in the winter and duct it into the entry way, or blow it outside in the summer—allowing for more efficient air conditioning. The cost of banking compressors in this way will usually carry an eight-month payback.

One should have maintenance contracts with the electrician, refrigeration air conditioner engineer, drainage/septic specialist, plumber, boiler engineer, and fire safety expert. Preventive maintenance can have an affect on fire, inside liability, and grounds insurance rates. If your facility looks good, you have the right to have an audit to reduce high insurance premiums.

When something breaks down, someone has to call the proper technician. While it seems reasonable that if the lights go out an employee would call the electrician, its best to leave nothing to chance. A list of possible problems, with the corresponding technicians' names, telephone numbers, and other information should be posted by every phone in the restaurant (except the pay phones). For example, in the plumbing category the list might read:

Problem	a. broken pipe
	b. flood from leaky pipes
	c. no hot water
	d. toilet or sink problems
Call	Ray's Plumbing 931-5825, ask for Carl.
	Home number: 931-4422

FIGURE 25

All technicians should be listed on a chart in this manner. This is an important means of expediting the repairs necessary for staying in business.

THE NEW FACILITY

For a new restaurant, my advice is to oversize services. For example, if your equipment and fixtures require 200 amps of service, have 400 amps of service installed. The initial expense should be factored into your start-up costs. The theory here is that if additional electrical equipment is required, and the original service cannot handle a bigger load, there will not only be the expense of running new conduits and lines, but also the expense of replacing the old service. Electricians have told me that electrical motors have a longer lifetime if the power is adequate at all times. When motors are forced to work harder, they wear out quickly, and changing service to expand a restaurant can also lead to down time for new installation.

I believe in oversizing all utility services. For water service, the cost of installing a six-inch service compared to the cost for a two-inch service is minimal. Go for the bigger service; you might need it! This is also true of natural gas.

If a restaurant is not located on a sewer line, an adequate septic system is required. The system should be in a location accessible to septic service trucks, but as far away from the public entry as possible. When the cover of a septic tank is removed the odor can have the intensity of two dead skunks—and linger just as long. Location of the septic system may not seem to be the responsibility of the restaurant owner: I have found that architects and septic engineers seldom address these problems in their plans. They don't have to live with that location. The restaurant does.

The septic system should be as large as the budget will allow. This way, solid waste will not have to be disposed of as often and service charges will be held to a minimum. In a new facility, prevention of problems should be a prime consideration. This fosters a smoother-running establishment.

FACILITY CONSIDERATIONS

Insulation, proper ventilation, and weather-stripping have been a part of energy conservation since the early seventies. Heating and air conditioning costs for restaurants have risen more rapidly than any other budget item. Fortunately, excessive energy costs can be prevented through good planning and innovative energy-saving measures.

Banking heat-rendering compressors is one method of cooling down the kitchen, and a cool kitchen is important for a number of reasons. Every kitchen needs a flow of air in order to have properly functioning cooking equipment. Gas stoves run efficiently when there is a well-balanced air distribution in a room. Refrigeration runs better when kitchen temperatures are lowered.

All of this can be accomplished by having proper ventilation ducts to take heated air from the kitchen and to replace it with fresh, outside air. At a cost that is not prohibitive, you can have a comfortable, energy-efficient kitchen. Contact an air conditioning or ventilation expert for the correct advice on how to accomplish this. When equipment is running efficiently, there are savings both in energy costs and repair costs. When there is excess heat in a kitchen, that heat makes its way to the serving areas, increasing air-conditioning expenses. In this era of volatile energy prices, energy efficiency is a must. "You forgot to turn off the oven last night," is a statement constantly heard in restaurants throughout the world. Make sure it applies to your restaurant as infrequently as possible.

A kitchen manager should post a checklist with designated times for turning on and turning off all equipment in the facility. It is common to have a food warmer or steam table on long after there is no longer food in it. I have seen tremendous energy waste in restaurants where appliances and equipment, too, are left on long after they have been in use. On a daily basis, this wears down equipment and wastes money.

Cooks, salad makers, and dishwashers must be reminded periodically that the equipment they are using is both fragile and costly to run. At the end of the day or at the end of their shift, they must be responsible for the proper care of the equipment, whether that means shutting it off, lowering its temperature or emptying it. These duties must be specific and known to everyone.

Sanitation

An unkept building can precipitate tremendous internal and public relations problems for any food-service facility. Holes and cracks in walls, ceilings, and floors can allow rodents or insects in. Accordingly, there should be a periodic check of the whole facility to detect any kind of infestation. Synthetic chemical technology has given us a wide range of products that can be applied easily to any crack or hole.

A periodic check should include all areas of the building. Look on top of, behind, and underneath all equipment and furnishings. Remember, rats usually don't knock on the front door when they want to come in.

Clean equipment is essential for good food. The kitchen staff should take equipment apart and clean it on a regular basis. My mother used to say that dirt crawls. If the dining areas of a restaurant are constantly polished and cleaned, yet the kitchen is dirty, the grime will spread, true to my mother's word. A waitress who walks on a greasy or dirty kitchen floor will track that dirt onto the carpeting in the dining room.

While the majority of cleaning is done by employees, a successful restaurant must have some help from outside, expert cleaning maintenance contractors, including:

1. Air ventilation contractors, to insure the upkeep of heating and air-conditioning ducts and smoke-eater systems.

2. A cleaning company, to do the very deep carpet cleaning that can only be done with sophisticated machinery.

3. A drain cleaning company to clean all waste drains and grease traps periodically.

4. A professional exterminator to curb any infestation.

5. A trash or garbage disposal company to haul away waste. (Once again, I believe in oversizing when a dumpster is used.)

HUMAN TRAFFIC PATTERNS

Part of facility management is concern for the traffic patterns so vital to restaurant activity. Entrance and exit plans that control the flow of customers should not conflict with employee movement, and vice-versa. In other words, the dumpster should be placed so that someone emptying trash does not cross paths with customers arriving at or departing from the restaurant. Likewise, the busing of dirty dishes should be planned so it does not interfere with the avenues customers will use to visit restrooms or enter dining areas.

The receiving dock should be as far away from the entrance as possible. Good architects, unfortunately, are not always good at traffic control. The prospective restaurateur should make every effort to communicate the idea of traffic flow to the architect and to anyone involved in planning the restaurant. (This is one of the concerns mentioned in the postmenu planning section.) Kitchen traffic must work much like street and auto traffic to be efficient. The same is true when considering customer movements.

Most states have passed or are considering passing handicap barrier laws. Access for the handicapped is a prime concern to new restaurant facilities, which generally have to comply with the new architectural codes.

Easy accessibility is a worthwhile cultural consideration and also benefits the restaurant by providing a broader range of customers. Wider entrances and foyer space is required to accommodate wheelchair customers and traffic patterns must incorporate the movements of handicapped customers.

Safety

It goes without saying that management must create a safe environment for both customer and employee.

The engineered fire production system, which is activated by excessive heat, must be constantly checked by trained specialists. Proper fire extinguishers should be placed strategically throughout the facility.

Lighting must be adequate in all areas. Backup lights and bulbs should always be in storage. Walkways must be clear and accessible to all patrons, including the handicapped.

Clearly defined exits are required by law in most states; the exits must always be uncluttered in case of an emergency.

The facility is an integral part of a restaurant and its success. Management must place a high priority on all aspects of its upkeep.

CONCLUSION

I HAVE SHARED MY OBSERVATIONS AND EXPERIENCES WITH YOU IN the hope that they will help lead you to success in this exciting field. My guess is that the ideas and concepts in this book will benefit you most if you review them occasionally. Monitor your progress against the goals and targets I've established perhaps every three months. We have covered enough ground together that it should come as no surprise to you if a few points slip past despite your best intentions.

Whatever you do, don't read the book once, nodding your head in agreement, and then fail to follow through. Get the very most you can out of Your New Restaurant. Hold your restaurant to the highest standards, and work constantly to improve it. Success will follow, as it has for the many clients for whom I have done consulting work.

Good luck!

Other Adams Publishing Books

The Adams Business Advisors

- *Accounting for the New Business*: How to do your own accounting simply, easily, and accurately. $12.95. Christopher R. Malburg

- *The All-in-One Business Planning Guide*: How to create cohesive plans for marketing, sales, operations, finance, and cash flow. $10.95. Christopher R. Malburg

- *Buying Your Own Business*: identifying opportunities, analyzing true value, negotiating the best terms, closing the deal. $12.95. Russell Robb

- *Do-It-Yourself Advertising, Direct Mail, and Publicity*: Ready-to-use templates, worksheets, and samples for creating ads, direct mail pieces, press releases, and other promotional items. $17.95. Sarah White and John Woods

- *Entrepreneurial Growth Strategies*: Strategic planning, restructuring alternatives, marketing tactics, financing options, acquisitions, and other ways to propel the new venture forward. $10.95. Lawrence W. Tuller

- *Exporting, Importing, and Beyond*: A handbook for growing businesses selling products and services in global markets. $10.95. Lawrence W. Tuller

- *Managing People*: Creating the team-based organization; guidelines for total group participation, employee empowerment, and organization development. $12.95. Darien McWhirter

- *Marketing Magic*: Innovative and proven ideas for finding customers, making sales, and growing your business. $10.95. Don Debelak

- *The Personnel Policy Handbook for Growing Companies*: How to create comprehensive guidelines, procedures, and checklists. $10.95. Darien McWhirter

- *Service, Service, Service*: The growing business' secret weapon; innovative and proven ideas for getting and keeping customers. $10.95. Steve Albrecht

- *Selling 101*: A course for business owners and non-sales people. Includes: finding leads, cold calling, handling objections, closing sales, growing sales. $12.95. Michael T. McGaulley

- *The Small Business Legal Kit*: ready-to-use forms, agreements, and contracts for small businesses. $17.95. J.W. Dicks

- *The Small Business Valuation Book*: Easy-to-use techniques for determining fair price, resolving disputes, and minimizing taxes. $10.95. Lawrence W. Tuller

- *Winning the Entrepreneur's Game*: How to start, operate, and be successful in a new or growing business. $10.95. David E. Rye

If you cannot find these titles at your favorite retail outlet, you may order them directly from the publisher. BY PHONE: Call 1-800-872-5627 (in Massachusetts 617-767-8100). We accept Visa, Mastercard, and American Express. $4.50 will be added to your total order for shipping and handling. BY MAIL: Write out the full title of the books you'd like to order and send payment, including $4.50 for shipping and handling to: Adams Publishing, 260 Center Street, Holbrook, MA 02343. 30-day money-back guarantee.